Artificial Rock Waterfalls

*Rock Making Techniques
For the Professional
and the Hobbyist*

J. ERIK KINKADE

GRANITE CANYON
PUBLICATIONS

GRANITE CANYON
PUBLICATIONS   SAN 254-640X

Second edition
First hardback edition published 2002

10 9 8 7 6 5 4 3 2

Library of Congress Cataloging-in-Publication Data

Kinkade, J. Erik
     Artificial Rock Waterfalls: rock making
     techniques for the professional and the
     hobbyist
     J. Erik Kinkade
         p.   cm.
     ISBN 0-9720036-5-7
     1. Water Features in Landscape Architecture.
     I. Kinkade, Erik   II. Title

SB475.8 .K56   2002   2002091611
714-DC21

Questions regarding the content and/or ordering of this book
should be addressed to:

Rock and Water
www.rockandwater.com
2631 West Bennett
Springfield, MO 65807
Information: (417) 848-2829

Printed in China
Through Overseas Printing Corporation
Design by   J. Erik Kinkade
Edited by   George N. Baldwin
                Martha E. Kinkade

Creating a Private Paradise with Artificial Rock Waterfalls

Here is a book which may be as useful to professional pool and spa builders as it is to the backyard hobbyist. *Artificial Rock Waterfalls, Rock Making Techniques* provides a wealth of knowledge gained from many years of hands-on experience in building artificial rock features.

An accomplished artificial rock artist, J. Erik Kinkade, has built water features and exhibits in every corner of the United States. Kinkade offers the knowledge that took years to acquire, through trial and error and by learning from other rock artists. Until now, there has been no instructional book on the subject of such widespread interest and industry.

Carefully designed to aid the builder, this *Complete Construction Guide to Artificial Rock Waterfalls* is a book worthy of its subject—creating fantasy environments for fun or for profit.

Artwork by David Kallemyn

Cascading waterfall,
GRFC Panels & Boulders
Supplied by Rock and Water
Creations

This book is dedicated to everyone who has the vision of creating a waterfall paradise, for themselves or for profit.

Table of Contents

Preface   *viii*

PART 3

————————————————

BUILDING THE ROCK

Waterfall in L.A. Zoo Habitat,
by Rock and Water Creations

Preface

Artificial rock making has been around for decades, but it was not until rock makers began using flexible molds of actual rock faces that the fabrication of rock progressed to a new level of realism. Artificial rock features created by this technique of rock making have been incorporated into zoo habitats, theme parks, museums, homes, and they are all very convincing imitations of actual rock formations. This superior grade of artificial rock has captured the imagination of designers as well as the public worldwide. Nature based models of rock have been used to create organic landscaping features for a variety of locations around the world and their high level of quality has set new standards for the industry.

Now you will have an opportunity to acquire the skills and knowledge to build your own artificial rock paradise—however large or small you desire it to be. You will have the ability to enhance any environment so that it reflects those elements of nature that all will admire.

This book offers the reader alternate ways of approaching rock making tasks, so small jobs can be constructed at home without the use of large equipment. At the same time, technical information is included for those readers who want more in-depth instruction in building artificial rock. Once you have a clear understanding of the principles of rock making as outlined in this text, you will be limited only by your imagination, your enthusiasm and your budget.

Designing, planning and constructing your own artificial rock feature will reward you on many levels for years to come. Humans have been interacting and shaping their environment for ages. Creating an artificial rock feature is just one more step toward building an inspirational environment that can be an important part of your home and lifestyle.

Waterfall and Hot Tub,
Chatsworth, CA
by Rock and Water Creations

Acknowledgments

Much of my thanks goes to my principal editor, colleague, and friend, George Baldwin. Without the generosity of his time and editorial skills, this book would have been a mediocre attempt at writing. His devotion as a friend has always been unwavering and his brilliance as a scholar is astounding.

My friend and colleague, Dave Kallemyn, deserves my thanks for all the beautiful drawings he did throughout the book. His style is one of the freshest and most beautiful styles I have ever come across in my career as an artist.

Thank you, Dr. Terry Chase, for your geological input and your willingness to help me whenever I asked for your assistance.

I would also like to thank my cousin Martha Kinkade for her editorial work and inspiration.

Thanks to all those who generously supplied photos, or who allowed their water features to be photographed and included in this book.

I greatly appreciate John Q. Hammons and his wonderful group of project managers who have afforded me many opportunities to work on their hotel water features.

Special thanks go to my Mother and Father for all the opportunities and support they have given me throughout my life.

Cascading Waterfall,
Palm Springs, CA
by Rock and Water Creations

Design

Part   1

CHAPTER ONE
Planning and Design

Let's face it, working with cement and steel can be hard work but the results can be spectacular and may last a lifetime. The creation of an artificial rock feature should not be an impulsive decision. Since a complete concrete rock formation is nearly impossible to move once it is constructed, the siting and the size of the rock feature requires a great deal of thought, as we shall see. A successful project, whose style, siting, construction and finishing have all been carefully considered, will generously reward the owner with a paradise that they may never want to leave.

The difficulty and amount of labor required to build an artificial rock waterfall is directly proportionate to its size. For this reason, if this is going to be your first construction project, you will probably want to start on a small scale. The first impulse for most people is to jump right in on that fantasy environment—the one they may have dreamt about for so long. Instead, break up that dream project into achievable sections, starting with a small section as your first project.

Your beginner or learning project should be able to stand on its own as a nice feature. Consider fabricating a small boulder along the edge of your pond or pool. It is possible, after experiencing the amount of work involved, that you may not choose to do anymore artificial rock work. You will not want to be "stuck" with a large unfinished structure with no likelihood of ever finishing it.

Waterfall and Koi pond for a private residence. The sweeping staircase was also done with artificial rock.
By Rock and Water

Waterfall and Koi pond design used as an entryway into an exclusive country club.

Designing the Rock and Water Feature

Much of the rock on Earth's surface was laid down in horizontal layers, either as sediment (like sandstone, shale, and limestone) or as flowing lava (like basalt). Very often these layers have vertical fractures that give the rocks a rather blocky appearance. When these rocks are exposed to prolonged periods of weathering, erosion by running water, or dissolution by organically derived acids, they may take on a more fractured and oddly shaped appearance. Still, they retain traces of their horizontal bedding.

Igneous rocks, like granite, were formed deep in the earth and were later exposed on the surface by erosion or mountain-building upheavals. While granite may sometimes appear layered because of horizontal fractures, it most commonly has a more massive, angular appearance. Its crystalline texture gives granite an overall granular and speckled look, often randomly cut by bands of darker or lighter material. Where granite has been weathered, it characteristically takes on a rounded pillow-like look.

Metamorphic rocks (like gneiss, quartzite, schist, and marble) are formed when sedimentary or igneous rocks are subjected to intense heat and pressure during tectonic movements of the earth's crust. These rocks are highly variable in appearance, but they usually display banded patterns which more often than not are contorted into convoluted ribbons. Weathered surfaces usually reflect this layering, often more vertical than horizontal. Metamorphic rocks are commonly cut by numerous fractures that divide them into large chunks. As in all rocks, these fracture lines are points where weathering takes place most rapidly and so they are usually accentuated by prominent indentations.

Because of their varying composition, rocks have different degrees of hardness and resistance to weathering. Alternating layers of limestone and softer shale, for example, often take on a layer-cake appearance with harder limestone beds protruding out over inset beds of shale. Climate greatly affects the way rocks weather. In the dry American West, limestone is the prominent "cap rock," more resistant to weathering than sandstone, that more easily disintegrates from abrasive, blowing sand. The West also has many lava flows that are even more resistant than limestone. In the more humid American East, limestone tends to dissolve away from acids created by abundant organic ground cover, while sandstone forms prominent caps. Therefore waterfalls in the East most often flow over a sandstone formation, while in the West the ledge is commonly limestone or basalt.

When considering your design for a rock formation, take inspiration from the rock in the local area. Consider doing some field research; take some pictures of nearby rock formations for later use in creating your artificial rock feature. Even if it is just a small pond waterfall you are creating, think about how the rock was formed and where it might have come from. Using rock formations that match the local area rock makes it appear more natural.

A good source for images of waterfall shapes and sizes is the Internet, with a simple search for waterfall pictures. You will no doubt find more than enough images online to help you in your design. When you look at a large real waterfall, remember that you can make yours smaller; it will still look natural, as rock tends to fracture and look the same at different scales.

Siting the Rock and Water Feature

In deciding where to place a rock feature or waterfall, sit for a while in the proposed location and imagine where movement, noise or reflection could add a new

Waterfall in the winter, GFRC Panels and Boulders Supplied by Rock and Water Creations

Plan view for private residence. This view shows waterfall and koi pond with stream leading to the lower pond area. The finished water feature is shown on page 2.

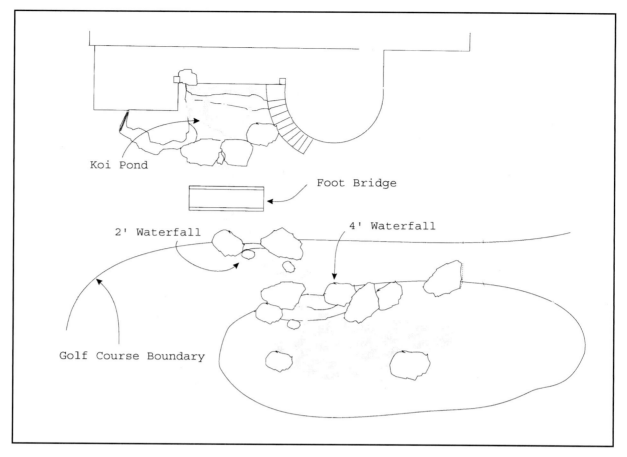

Koi Pond

Foot Bridge

2' Waterfall

4' Waterfall

Golf Course Boundary

dimension to the area. There is a real bonus to any rock feature which can be seen easily from the house, but in certain cases this may not be important.

There are several considerations to bear in mind when choosing a site. These are in part aesthetic considerations and in broad terms they ought to include some concern for the style of the architecture and the surrounding natural landscape. You will also need to consider the practical aspects of the site, such as the lay of the land, the accessibility for trucks and equipment, as well as the ease of serviceability, when building a water feature.

Electricity is another important consideration; it may be required for pumps, heating and lighting. If the proposed site is some distance from its nearest source, you should consider the cost of taking power to the site. Similarly, in water features where frequent filling or "topping off" from the domestic water supply is

necessary, it is wise to ensure that this is reasonably close. Always check that the pool excavation will not damage any existing water pipes, electric cables or drains, before starting the construction. Always excavate with caution.

It is vital to make the rock feature as safe as possible. Whether you are building a dry rock feature or a waterfall, it is important to remember the safety of children, adults, and pets. The idea of an artificial rock feature or pond may have to be abandoned or postponed by parents of young children as the precautions necessary to make the rock feature or pool totally safe may over-ride its aesthetic value.

A dry rock feature can be an irresistible draw for climbing. And, just as when hiking in Nature, a fall from rock cliffs only a few feet high can be deadly.

There is significant concern for safety when electrical equipment (submersible pumps or lighting) is installed in a water feature. Water and electricity can be a potentially lethal mix. No matter how simple the installation may appear, it is important to use approved electrical fittings and equipment, and to consult, or better still, to employ a qualified licensed electrician. As an extra precaution, it is strongly recommended that you install a contact circuit breaker where electrical equipment is used in, or near the water. These devices are simple to connect, and in the event of any electricity leakage, they cut off the current within 30 milliseconds to protect against severe electric shock.

The Plan View

Start with a simple drawing, as though you were looking down on your water feature or rock formation. Draw an outline of where the rock will go including some existing landmarks, such as the house, trees, or the shape of the existing pool or pond where the rock will go. This is called the plan view. The illustration on page 5 is a good example of a plan view initially used in developing a design for an artificial rock waterfall and koi pond.

Use your plan view to work out walking paths, edges, and widths of the rock formations. Include the pond or swimming pool edge if you are doing a water feature. If you will be including lighting, speakers, or plumbing fixtures into the artificial rock, these should also be noted and positioned on the plan view. It is always a good idea to work in a scale, that is to say, every item drawn on the plan view is proportionate and measured equally using a pre-established scale, such as: 1/4 inch is equal to one foot.

Using a scale means taking measurements of the actual area and using those measurements to translate the drawing onto a smaller format, such as a piece of paper. The size of your paper will determine the size of the scale you want to use. Architects' rulers or scales are widely available at any office supply, but make sure you get a scale that will work for

A typical elevation view showing the layers involved in the construction.

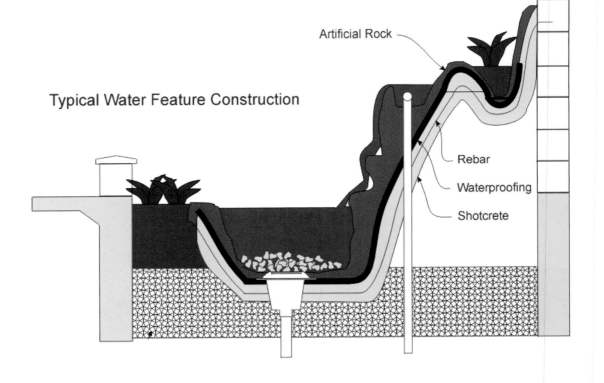

Typical Water Feature Construction

Artificial Rock

Rebar

Waterproofing

Shotcrete

Concept drawing for private residence. Finished water feature is shown on page 2. The pump room was located inside the large section of rock to the left, accessed through a discrete door hidden from view. Stairs were also incorporated into the rock feature.

you; typically a 3/4", 1/2",1/4", 1/8" scale is the best.

To assist you with your measurements, use the corner of the house or a tree as your anchor or starting point for taking the field measurements. All measurements will be made from this anchor point. Using an architect's scale, reduce that area down so it will fit on your page, that is, 1/4" on the page is equal to 1' of measurement on the site of the formation. Start on the page with the placement of the anchor point and scale all your measurements onto the page. If you draw it to scale you will always be correct in the proportions of the rock feature, as it relates to the surrounding elements. You could also use grid paper to lay out your plan view. Grid papers are widely available at office supply or craft stores, and can assist with accuracy since each square of the grid paper can represent a set scale of measurement. For example, one 1/4" square might be a one foot measurement in full size.

The Elevation View

The plan view shows the rock feature from above and translates your ideas into an outline map for use in laying out the formation. The elevation drawing is used to show the vertical elements of the rock formation. Since it would be difficult to show all the twists and turns of the formation on one sheet of paper, the drafting standard is to draw a line through part of the plan view of the formation, with an arrow pointing to one side of the line indicating a view for an elevation drawing. For example, imagine you were small enough to stand on your plan view page. Wherever you are standing, the direction toward which you are looking is what the dissecting line and arrow are indicating. The dissecting line would be from shoulder to shoulder and the arrow would be the direction toward which you were facing. You can do as many elevation views as you think you will need to translate your ideas. This allows someone else to be able to see your ideas and it will also give you a guide for building the

Concept drawing for a 15' X 25' three-tiered waterfall for a dance club. The waterfalls incorporate fiber-optic lighting which illuminates the waterfalls and even adds a glow to the pond. The light color continually changes to several colors. The mechanical room is located inside the rock structure on the left through a standard door textured to look like rock.

formation. On page 6 there is a good example of an elevation view. Remember that the elevation view should also be drawn to scale, and in most cases it should match the scale used for the plan view. If different scales are used for the plan view and elevation view, you should note the scale used just below the drawing.

Concept Drawing

If you have drawing skills, you may want to do a concept drawing. This is basically a snapshot or picture of what the finished rock feature will look like from a certain point of view. If you don't have the skills needed to draw such an elaborate concept drawing as the one example above, even a rough drawing can say volumes and help you formulate your ideas about what the rock feature should look like. If you are doing a commercial job, you will want a professional drawing so clients will know what the finished product will look like. This can reduce the potential miscommunications about the finished product and it can help tremendously in bidding and selling a project to the client. Most professional artists can take a simple sketch or outline, and with

possibly one or two revisions, draw a good example. Make sure you see previous examples of the artist's work, especially black and white pen art, before contracting them. You will want to establish a price with the artist beforehand, as well.

Pricing the Rock and Water Feature

Now that you have your ideas and designs drawn to scale and on paper in the form of the Plan View, Elevation View, and Concept Drawing, you can begin to catch glimpses of the square footage involved in the project. The more accurate you can estimate the square footage, the more assured you will be in meeting the budget or winning a bid.

Given the natural shape of any rock with its uneven sides, the undercuts and tops, certain difficulties arise as you try to estimate its square footage. One good strategy for estimating a job is breaking the rock feature into general geometric shapes. Squares work well because they are the least complex shape for determining square footage and it helps one visualize how the structure will take its shape. You find the square feet of a square by multiplying the height times the width which gives the total area of the square.

Once you establish the square footage of your project, you can begin the price estimating. Breakdown the water feature project into several levels of pricing, each with a different cost. Consider using the following pricing structure when bidding a job: support structure, hand-carved rock surface, waterproofed surface, cast-rock-panel surface, pond shell or mud-like surface, and mechanical components. All but the mechanical components are bid off the square footage figure. The cost of the mechanical system may vary widely from job to job and requires a more customized approach.

The cost of a rock feature can be likened to that of building a basement in a home and decorating it. Essentially, the same materials are used and many of the same processes. Basements need to be water-proofed and strong, as do artificial rock waterfalls. And, as with a wet basement, a leaky waterfall can be a difficult challenge to fix.

At the time this book was written (in 2002) the industry standard for pricing was $25 - $45 per square foot for bidding a project. A 20% additional square footage would be added for profit. The price would fluctuate from the hand-carved rock to the more costly water-proofed areas. Don't forget to include the price of precast panels (precast panels are discussed on page 51) if this is how you will create the rock. They all require different amounts of labor and materials which affect the square footage cost.

In order to get an accurate look at what it will cost, the plumbing system, as well as the mechanical components in the pond and pump room, all need to be individually priced and then added together, along with the estimated labor needed to complete the project. You may want to take your pump room layout to a few plumbers and get bids from them—especially if plumbing and mechanical component installation are not part of your experience.

Summary

One nice thing about using cement for artificial rock is that you can always add to it easily; removing material is not as easy and can involve a great deal of expensive effort. The more effort you put into the design and planning, the less likely you will need to change the work after you have it "roughed in." Look to nature for inspiration in your design, but look to your plans and elevations for guidance in its construction.

Finished three-tiered waterfall with fiber-optic lighting of the waterfalls. The Twilite Zone Dance Club in St. Robert, MO, by Rock and Water

Cascading Waterfall,
Montacito, CA by
Rock and Water Creations

Operations *Part 2*

CHAPTER TWO
The Water Works

Think of the water feature as a living organism; the mechanical system is what keeps it alive and functioning properly. This mechanical system can also be referred to as "the waterworks" which is made up of plumbing, electrical, and also the equipment needed to make the water feature work. This can include: pipes, pumps, filtration system, sterilization, valving, and equipment housing.

When designing an artificial rock water feature, such as a pond or waterfall, you must think about the placement of the plumbing and electrical equipment before beginning the construction of the artificial rock. Whether you are planning an outdoor water feature or an indoor feature, the proper plumbing and electri-

cal needs must be done first.

Once the design for the plumbing and electrical components is done, you can excavate for the pond and mechanical trenches, laying plumbing and electrical conduit in trenches, or buried along the side of the pond. The pipes and conduit will be brought out of the ground or "stubbed up" at the appropriate place, as indicated on your plan view. All elements should be included. This can include bringing up plumbing and conduit for drains, skimmers, jets, underwater electrical boxes, lights, overflow, and water level sensors.

The Mechanical System

Several decisions regarding your proposed system need to be made early on.

Mechanical Considerations:

- Do you want to be able to drain the water feature easily?

- Where will the drained water feature water go? Many cities require that chemically treated water be drained into the sanitary system, and not the storm system.

- How will you start and stop the water feature?

- Will winter and freezing temperatures damage fish, or equipment?

- Where will the equipment be housed?

Use the component checklist to verify that all the needed components have been evaluated and/or included in your water feature design.

- How big of a waterfall do you want? This will determine how big a pump you will need.

- Do you want the water feature to be self-filling with makeup water for evaporation?

- Do you want underwater lights?

- Do you want a skimmer?

- Do you want benthic jets to help the circulation in the water feature?

- Will you have fish, or will it be a chemically treated fountain?

- Do you want spa controls, if building a spa?

- What size of pipe do you need? This is determined by the amount of water flow and pump size.

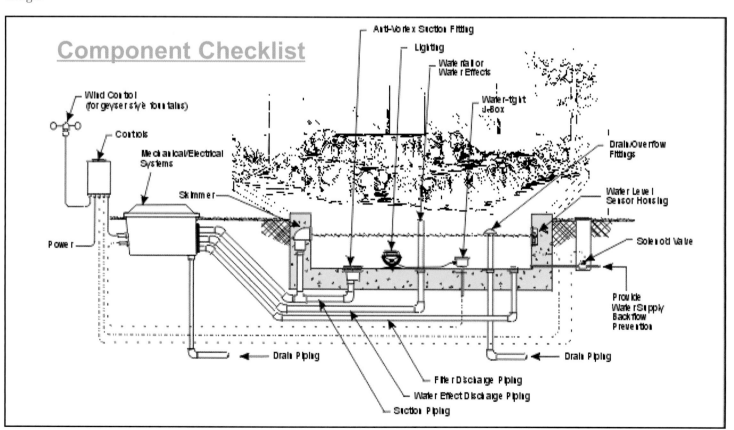

Component Checklist

Wind Control (for geyser style fountains)
Controls
Mechanical/Electrical Systems
Power
Skimmer
Anti-Vortex Suction Fitting
Lighting
Waterfall or Water Effects
Water-tight J-Box
Drain/Overflow Fittings
Water Level Sensor Housing
Solenoid Valve
Provide Water Supply Backflow Prevention
Drain Piping
Filter Discharge Piping
Water Effect Discharge Piping
Suction Piping

Waterfall at the elevators in the Sheraton Hotel, Sioux Falls, SD. Rock was created with molds taken from the local area's quartzite rock formations.
By Rock and Water

Make sure you address all of these questions in the beginning, because once the artificial rock is done, it is very difficult to add to it (or subtract from it) the forgotten, miscalculated or overlooked mechanical items.

Once you have addressed the plumbing and electrical concerns, you are ready to begin the design of the mechanical system.

Locating the Mechanical System

If the rock feature is big enough, consider including an access door to the interior of the rock feature. Mechanical and electrical components can be housed inside the rock feature, providing a space to hide pumps, filters, heaters, electrical panels, and spa equipment. Be sure the access door is properly sized for easy entry, and that it will meet local electrical codes. This is an ideal place for all the equipment, since it will be hidden and also close by.

Another option is to bury a mechani-

cal pit near the rock water feature with an access lid or port for entry. This location allows for a flooded suction at the pump, which is always good for the pump. One drawback is the possibility of

Access door to the interior of the rock feature. Pumps, filters, valves, and plumbing will be housed, out-of-sight, inside the rock.

14

flooding the pit and ruining equipment. Include some way of draining the mechanical vault, either with a float valve attached to a sump pump, or with a drain to a gravel pit below the vault.

Ideally, an interior framed room is best. However, unless it is all new construction, this can create a whole new set of challenges, such as getting the plumbing and electrical components into the room. You will also want the room to have a floor drain capable of handling substantial water flow. Distance from the water feature is an important consideration, since the farther away the mechanical site is, the larger the pipes and pumps that are required will need to be.

Many pond kits do not need a mechanical room, since they work off a skimmer and bog filtration system with a submersible pump located in the skimmer. These systems are fine for home use and some commercial applications; however, it is preferable to have the pump and controls in an easily accessible area. Many commercial jobs have above

ground pumps and controls in mechanical rooms. An easily accessible mechanical area will make servicing the water feature much more enjoyable, and in turn, the water feature will probably be taken care of better over the long term.

Water Flow Considerations

It is difficult to produce bad results when working with natural looking rock and the water that flows over it. Even a small amount of water running over a natural rock looks good. However, as with everything, you will want to consider a few important factors that will affect the results when designing the size and flow of the waterfall. Making good decisions in the design phase can save countless hours of frustration when trying to get a waterfall to splash less, create less noise, or have more "presence."

Shopping mall fountain with bronze sculpture of boy playing with an otter.

Design for a private home spa. The heated spa, was designed with jets and lights which were incorporated into the artificial rock.

Volume of Flow

The flow of the waterfall can be controlled by the valve at the discharge side of the pump. What you want, is for the pump to be neither too big nor too small for the optimum flow. One way to help imagine the optimum flow of a waterfall, is a simple rule: five gallons of flow per foot of weir. Weir is the length of the edge that the waterfall spills over. For example, a five foot span of weir would require 25 gallons a minute flow rate (5' x 5 gallons per foot = 25 gallons per minute flow) to achieve the desired look. So, you would need a pump capable of delivering 1500 gallons per hour (gph) or 25 gallons per minute (gpm). This will provide a fast and constant flow over the edge of the waterfall. If you want a more "lazy" waterfall, you will want to reduce the gallons per foot accordingly. Of course, this does not take into consideration "head loss" which we will cover in the plumbing section.

Electrical expenses may play a part in determining the flow of the waterfall. The waterfall owner may be shocked with his first electrical bill, if the cost is not looked at in the early stages. You can easily determine how much a pump will cost to run, using this formula:

[pump draws_(__)_amps x volts (115/220/208)]/ 1000] x cost per KwH (from electrical bill) x 24 (hours) x 30.4 days per average month = average cost per month

Example formula:
A 1/4 horse pump on a medium size waterfall draws 2.9 amps (printed on the outside of the pump) and runs on 115 v. power divided by 1000, multiplied by the cost per kilowatt hour (found on an electrical bill) multiplied by the number of hours in a day (24) multiplied by the yearly average of days in a month (30.4) will give you the average monthly cost. That

is, 2.9 x115 =333.5 / 1000=0.3335 x .0697 (substitute your KwH charge) =.0232 x 24 = .5568 x 30.4 = $16.92 per month. Using this formula, you can see how two small pumps that draw less amps, in place of one large pump that draws large amps, can save a significant amount of money over the life of the pumps. It does require a larger initial cost, however.

Splash

Splashing is one of those natural occurrences that can be difficult to "control" if it presents a problem.

If you have a large pond, and plenty of room on either side of the waterfall, or if your waterfall flow is small, you may not need to worry. But if the waterfall is likely to splash walkways or splash outside the water containment area, you can loose significant amounts of water and possibly cause "slip hazards." If the water feature is indoors, there may be little or no allowance for splash.

There are very few "rules of thumb" for determining the area of splash. You should allow—at minimum —the height of the waterfall on sides and front, as a guide to determine the splash radius. In most cases, it will splash much farther than anticipated. Even small sprays of water can drench an area during a 24 hour period. I have gone so far as to build a plywood "mock-up" of the waterfall in order to determine the splash area. You can experiment with pouring a bucket of water from the desired height of the waterfall into another body of water on the ground to get another perspective. But in the end, it is safer to assume that you will have twice the height of the waterfall as the splash area.

Noise

You may not consider the beautiful sound of running water as "noise" but it can become a noise if it is the only sound one can hear. A close by neighbor, or someone near the waterfall wanting to hear another speak, may find the sound to be a nuisance. It is possible you will lose other natural sounds, such as the birds singing—which most people like to hear, as well. An indoor water feature that is too loud is definitely a noise.

Try to imagine the desired flow of water and the level of sound that it will create. This will also determine the amount of flow for you.

Plumbing

A piping installation consists of pipe, fittings and valves. Normally, friction loss through a fitting is described as being equivalent to friction loss through a cer-

Typical piping trench with pipes laid in the trench for various parts of the water feature. Underground piping must be installed before any construction is done. The buried depth of the piping is critical to insure that pipe is not damaged during construction.

Friction Loss In Pipe

CARRYING CAPACITY AND FRICTION LOSS
FOR SCHEDULE 40 THERMOPLASTIC PIPE

Gallons Per Minutes	1/2 in. Velocity Ft. Per Second	1/2 in. Friction Head Feet	3/4 in. Velocity Ft. Per Second	3/4 in. Friction Head Feet	1 in. Velocity Ft. Per Second	1 in. Friction Head Feet	1 1/4 in. Velocity Ft. Per Second	1 1/4 in. Friction Head Feet	1 1/2 in. Velocity Ft. Per Second	1 1/2 in. Friction Head Feet	2 in. Velocity Ft. Per Second	2 in. Friction Head Feet	2 1/2 in. Velocity Ft. Per Second	2 1/2 in. Friction Head Feet	3 in. Velocity Ft. Per Second	3 in. Friction Head Feet
1	1.13	2.08	0.63	0.51												
2	2.26	4.16	1.26	1.02	0.77	0.55	0.44	0.14	0.33	0.07						
5	5.64	23.44	3.16	5.73	1.93	1.72	1.11	0.44	0.81	0.22	0.49	0.066	0.30	0.038	0.22	0.015
7	7.90	43.06	4.43	10.52	2.72	3.17	1.55	0.81	1.13	0.38	0.69	0.11	0.49	0.051	0.31	0.021
10	11.28	82.02	6.32	20.04	3.86	6.02	2.21	1.55	1.62	0.72	0.98	0.21	0.68	0.09	0.44	0.03
15	**4 in**		9.48	42.64	5.79	12.77	3.31	3.28	2.42	1.53	1.46	0.45	1.03	0.19	0.66	0.07
20	0.51	0.03	12.65	72.34	7.72	21.75	4.42	5.59	3.23	2.61	1.95	0.76	1.37	0.32	0.88	0.11
25	0.64	0.04	**5 in**		9.65	32.88	5.52	8.45	4.04	3.95	2.44	1.15	1.71	0.49	1.10	0.17
30	0.77	0.06	0.49	0.02	11.58	46.08	6.63	11.85	4.85	5.53	2.93	1.62	2.05	0.68	1.33	0.23
35	0.89	0.08	0.57	0.03			7.73	15.76	5.66	7.36	3.41	2.15	2.39	0.91	1.55	0.31
40	1.02	0.11	0.65	0.03	**6 in**		8.84	20.18	6.47	9.43	3.90	2.75	2.73	1.16	1.77	0.40
45	1.15	0.13	0.73	0.04			9.94	25.10	7.27	11.73	4.39	3.43	3.08	1.44	1.99	0.50
50	1.28	0.16	0.81	0.05	0.56	0.02	11.05	30.51	8.08	14.25	4.88	4.16	3.42	1.75	2.21	0.60
60	1.53	0.22	0.97	0.07	0.67	0.03			9.70	19.98	5.85	5.84	4.10	2.46	2.65	0.85
70	1.79	0.30	1.14	0.10	0.79	0.04					6.83	7.76	4.79	3.27	3.09	1.13
75	1.92	0.34	1.22	0.11	0.84	0.05					7.32	8.82	5.13	3.71	3.31	1.28
80	2.05	0.38	1.30	0.13	0.90	0.05	**8 in**				7.80	9.94	5.47	4.19	3.53	1.44
90	2.30	0.47	1.46	0.16	1.01	0.06					8.78	12.37	6.15	5.21	3.98	1.80
100	2.56	0.58	1.62	0.19	1.12	0.08	0.65	0.03			9.75	15.03	6.84	6.33	4.42	2.18
125	3.20	0.88	2.03	0.29	1.41	0.12	0.81	0.035	**10 in**				8.55	9.58	5.52	3.31
150	3.84	1.22	2.44	0.40	1.69	0.16	0.97	0.04					10.26	13.41	6.63	4.63
175	4.48	1.63	2.84	0.54	1.97	0.22	1.14	0.055							7.73	6.16
200	5.11	2.08	3.25	0.69	2.25	0.28	1.30	0.07	0.82	0.027	**12 in**				8.83	7.88
250	6.40	3.15	4.06	1.05	2.81	0.43	1.63	0.11	1.03	0.035					11.04	11.83
300	7.67	4.41	4.87	1.46	3.37	0.60	1.94	0.16	1.23	0.05						
350	8.95	5.87	5.69	1.95	3.94	0.79	2.27	0.21	1.44	0.065	1.01	0.027				
400	10.23	7.52	6.50	2.49	4.49	1.01	2.59	0.27	1.64	0.09	1.16	0.04				
450			7.31	3.09	5.06	1.26	2.92	0.33	1.85	0.11	1.30	0.05				
500			8.12	3.76	5.62	1.53	3.24	0.40	2.05	0.13	1.45	0.06				
750					8.43	3.25	4.86	0.85	3.08	0.28	2.17	0.12				
1000					11.24	5.54	6.48	1.45	4.11	0.48	2.89	0.20				
1250							8.11	2.20	5.14	0.73	3.62	0.31				
1500							9.72	3.07	6.16	1.01	4.34	0.43				
2000									8.21	1.72	5.78	0.73				
2500									10.27	2.61	7.23	1.11				
3000											8.68	1.55				
3500											10.12	2.07				
4000											11.07	2.66				

Friction Loss In Fittings
Expressed in Equivalent Length of Straight Pipe, Feet

	1/2 in.	3/4 in.	1 in.	1 1/4 in.	1 1/2 in.	2 in.	3 in.	4 in.
Gate Valve (Full Open)	0.6	0.7	0.9	1.2	1.3	1.6	2.0	2.7
Elbow, 90 Degree	3.6	4.5	5.3	6.7	7.5	8.6	11.1	13.1
Elbow, 45 Degree	0.7	0.9	1.4	1.8	2.2	2.8	4.1	5.6
Tee (Straight Thru)	1.8	2.5	3.3	4.7	5.7	7.8	12.1	17.1
Tee Thru Side	4.3	5.4	6.7	8.8	10.0	12.1	17.1	21.2
Swing Check Valve	8.1	8.9	11.2	13.1	15.2	19.1	27.1	38.2

Typical plumbing system design. PVC pipe and fittings can be used in most systems making it much easier to plumb.

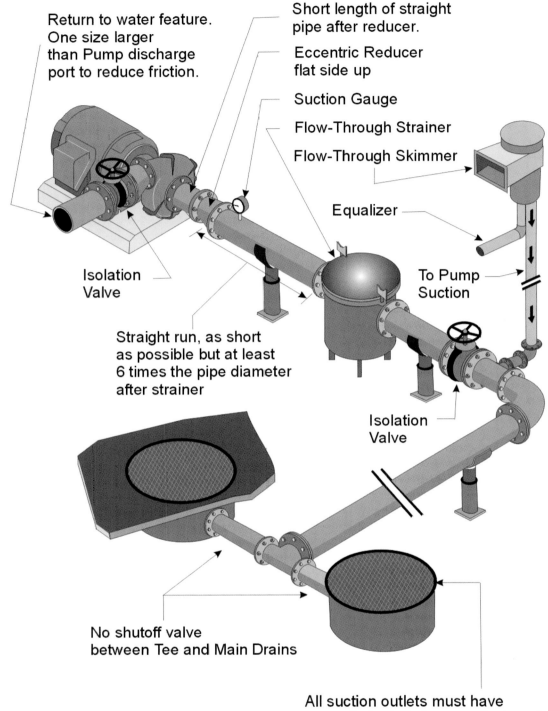

Return to water feature. One size larger than Pump discharge port to reduce friction.

Short length of straight pipe after reducer.

Eccentric Reducer flat side up

Suction Gauge

Flow-Through Strainer

Flow-Through Skimmer

Equalizer

To Pump Suction

Isolation Valve

Straight run, as short as possible but at least 6 times the pipe diameter after strainer

Isolation Valve

No shutoff valve between Tee and Main Drains

All suction outlets must have correctly installed, screw-fastened covers in place.

System Connection

tain number of linear feet of straight pipe. When calculating head loss through a piping system, add together the number of feet represented by all the different fittings that will be used in the system—use the chart on page 18 to get the number of feet for each fitting. Then add that number to the friction loss in linear feet of pipe. This will provide an estimate for the head loss figure that will be needed to determine the pump size. Data giving approximate friction losses in equivalent feet for a selection of PVC pipe fittings in different pipe sizes, as well as in straight lengths, are all given in the charts on page 18.

Piping

System piping should be at least one commercial pipe size larger than pump connections, and flow velocity should not exceed eight (8) feet per second.

NOTICE: Take care to align piping with pump case. Misalignment or excessive pipe strain can cause distortion of pump components resulting in rubbing, breakage, and reduced pump life.

Support the pipe so that no force is exerted on pump connections. Check the alignment as follows: With the pump shut down and isolation valves closed, remove pipe flange bolts. If the mating flanges come apart or shift, misalignment is present and is causing pressure on the connections. Adjust the pipe supports until flanges mate without any force. This procedure can be done throughout the piping system.

Refer to system connection diagram on page 19 for recommended practices in suction and discharge connections.

Mechanical system for a large aquarium and waterfall.

I. THREADED JOINTS
    A. Plastic to Plastic
        1. A dry male fitting should make up hand-tight about two-thirds (2/3) of the way into any female threaded connection.
        2. Use only the following plastic-to-plastic thread sealants. Teflon tape, 100% pure Teflon or Permatex #2. Use three (3) full clockwise turns of Teflon tape.
        3. Apply sealant to male thread only. Use liberal coats of either the 100% pure Teflon or Permatex #2. Use three (3) full clockwise turns of Teflon tape.
        4. Screw the fittings together hand-tight. Then one half (1/2) to one (1) more full turn using a strap wrench or small pipe wrench. You now have a good joint—stop.

    B. Plastic to Metal
        1. Be sure to clean or deburr any rough metal threads to prevent uneven covering of sealants or tearing of the tape.
        2. The same sealants are recommended as above.
        3. Avoid the use of a male metal threaded end into a female plastic thread, whenever possible.
            a. If heated water of any degree is involved, the different expansion rates could cause leaks.
            b. Tapered metal male fittings over-tightened into plastic female threads can create stresses that, though not immediately apparent, can cause fractures later.
        4. Screw the fittings together hand-tight. Then, one (1) more full turn using a strap wrench or a small pipe wrench. You now have a good joint—stop.

Note: Most common plumber's oil-base pipe dope compounds should not be used with plastic pipe, valves or fittings. Cracking or breaking of valves and fittings has been caused by the effects of some of these pipe dopes, failures occur shortly after use and over prolonged periods of time.

II. SOLVENT WELDING
        1. Avoid using the so-called all-purpose cements or spray can types. Here are the suggested solvent cements:
            a. To join ABS to ABS use Weld-on 771 "White"
            b. To join ABS to PVC use Weld-on 794 "Green"
            c. To join PVC to PVC use Weld-On 711 "Gray"
        2. Use a good cleaner product such as Weld-on C-65
        3. With a clean rag, liberally saturated with cleaner, wipe fitting socket and pipe end until they feel tacky.
        4. Quickly, while surfaces are tacky, brush on moderate coating of cement to the fitting socket and pipe end.
        5. Within 5 to 10 seconds, insert pipe, giving it a slight twist as it bottoms out.
        6. Hold joint for 5 to 10 seconds to prevent pipe from pushing out of socket.

Note: You can handle the pipe almost at once. Do not put any stress or twisting force on the joint for at least twenty (20) minutes. Do not pressurize for at least two (2) hours. A full 100% joint strength takes forty-eight (48) hours.

Concept drawing for a replicated Greek ruin with waterfall surrounding the ruin.

Plumbing Tips

Page 21 offers a few tips on how to plumb with plastic pipe and fittings, using threaded joints and /or solvent welding. There are many variations published on how to use plastics. The plumbing tips outlined here are recommended for piping systems normally encountered in the swimming pool and spa industry.

Pumps

The vast array of products available can make the design aspect of a water feature challenging. Many questions arise when selecting a pump that will meet your particular needs. You should answer these four questions first:

1. Is the pump meant to operate a fountain or waterfall?
2. Was it designed for continuous operation?
3. Does it have a filter, or can it pass debris?
4. Is it submersible, or can it be installed out of the water?

One can often observe pumps being operated in water features that are totally unsuitable for this task, due to the bearing technology and motor systems. Most of these pumps were developed as submersible drainage, or sump pumps. They were designed to empty reservoirs, cellars and sumps, but not for continuous operation. They have a very high power consumption rate and seldom last longer than 3000 operating hours.

For the purpose of this book we will look at two basic types of pumps used in water features: a centrifugal pump, and a submersible pump. A centrifugal pump is an out-of-the-water pump and works on high volume, low pressure. This kind of pump can be seen on most pool and spa systems. A submersible pump is in the water and is made for safe underwater operation.

Choosing a pump for a water feature should be based on a few job requirements. Desired flow, pumping height, and electrical costs are all factors that need to be considered. The higher the pump needs to push water, the less flow you are going to get out of that pump. You ought to have a pump that can create the desired look of the waterfall as well as turn the water over, through filtration in the pond or fountain, once an hour. High efficiency pumps will last longer and require less electricity. High efficiency pumps cost dramatically less over the long run, but they require a larger initial investment. The cost savings over the life of the pump can represent huge savings and should not be disregarded. See page 16 for electrical cost formulas.

Entrapment Protection

If you are building a fountain or spa that will be accessible to humans or animals, you must provide protection against the hazard of suction entrapment or hair entrapment and entanglement. To provide proper protection, at least two hydraulically balanced main drains, that is to say main drains installed in a "T" configuration, with covers for each suction line, must be used in the pool. The centers of the main drains (suction fittings) must be at least three feet apart. The system must be built so that it cannot operate with the pump drawing water from only one main drain. There must be at least two main drains connected to the pump whenever it is running. See Valves and Connections on page 19 for the proper layout of the system. These necessary precautions will assure a safe environment for having fun.

Summary

A large portion of the cost of the water feature will be in the mechanical system. However the mechanical system is no place to make budget cut backs. A good mechanical system will save everyone a lot of grief in the future if it is done correctly.

Any part of the mechanical system that you are not familiar with should be installed by an experienced professional. Hiring a professional, even if it is only for the first few water features you build, will teach you the proper way to do it yourself in the future.

Atrium Waterfall, Artificial granite created with molds taken from local area rock, by Rock and Water, Sioux Falls, SD Sheraton Hotel.

CHAPTER THREE

Water Treatment

Concept drawing for waterfall built against a dirt berm or hillside and flowing to a pond.

When designing the water treatment system, most water features will fall into one of two types of water treatment categories: biological or chemical. The biological type of treatment is used to create a living pond or water feature. The chemical system is used when it is important to protect the public from contaminations—nothing can grow in a chemically treated environment, including plants and fish.

We will discuss both systems in the following chapter; the intended use of the water feature will determine which system you choose to install.

Biological Filtration Systems

If you want to cultivate fish or amphibians in your water feature you must use a biological filtration system. The waste from the living creatures is what will "feed" the filtration system and keep the pond water clean.

Bio-Bead Filters

Bio-bead filters can take on many shapes and sizes and are used only for supporting a pond or fountain that has living organisms in it, such as fish or turtles. They all work under pressure, like a swimming pool filter, and some bio-bead filters use the same filter components as swimming pools do, except that they modify the interior workings to better promote the growth of healthy bacteria. The interior of the filter is filled with beads just as pool filters are filled with sand. The beads are designed to function naturally in the same way as (for example) the Great Barrier Reef. Thousands of little shapes or beads with holes capturing water borne particles and fish waste, grow and hold ammonia oxidizing and heterotropic bacteria. Heavy fish waste and tiny particles—even fine suspended solids—are trapped in the porous material while billions of nitrifying bacteria go to work, consuming organic mater and keeping the water clear.

Bio-bead filters are an excellent choice for out-of-the-pond filtration. They can be used in pump pits, and pump rooms. Some are designed to be buried, with just the controls above the ground. They offer a clean and dry way of maintaining a pond with fish. The key element that they require to function properly is the waste material from living organisms, such as fish.

One drawback to these filters is that waste-eating bacteria, inside the filter, will die without water and oxygen moving through the filter. When the biological colony inside the filter dies, a large amount of toxic hydrogen sulfide is created, which can be deadly to the fish population. If the flow of the water is "off" or obstructed for more than 4-5 minutes, the colony of bacteria in the filter will begin to die. Some systems have air injectors that switch "on" when the water flow stops, to keep the filter alive until the water resumes its flow. Without this, you run the risk of having a power outage that is "off" long enough to kill the filter, but comes back "on" and injects the pond with deadly hydrogen sulfide.

If you do use a bio-bead filter, make sure you backwash out the harmful agents after a filter has been turned "off" for an extended period of time. Once the harmful agents are washed out from the filter, and it is supplied with a continuous flow of water, the colony of bacteria will return very quickly.

For even cleaner, crystal clear water, a

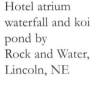

Hotel atrium waterfall and koi pond by Rock and Water, Lincoln, NE

standard sand filter can be added, next to the bio-bead filter, to filter those particles that get by the bio-bead filter.

Bog Filters

A bog filter is used at the head of a waterfall or stream. The return pond water is pumped to the bottom of a container that is filled with porous material such as lava stone. As the unfiltered water moves through the filter medium to the top of the container, its waste and debris are deposited in the filter medium.

Bog filters are, in most cases, the most effective way to filter large outdoor biological water features. A bog filter can be designed to have a waterfall ledge for the water exiting the filter, which can make it an easy and discrete way to incorporate the filter system into the water feature. Bogs are also a great place to have aquatic plants that voraciously feed on the organic material deposited in the filter. This will usually maintain crystal clear water.

The drawback to a bog filter is the maintenance required to remove the lava rock, or filter medium, and clean the container as well as the filter medium of non-organic debris, such as sand and dirt.

Sterile Filtration Systems

If you do not want fish or aquatic plants in your water feature and you want to control the growth of algae, you will probably want to use a sand filter with chemical sterilization, just as you would in a swimming pool.

Sand Filters

Sand filters are used on fountains and water features that do not include fish or aquatic plants or where the water is intended for safe human contact. It is not that people typically drink water from a decorative fountain; however, nearly everyone is compelled to dip his or her hand into a fountain thereby transferring bacteria into the water, and possibly pick-

Artificial rock waterfall and koi pond. Epcott Center, FL, Fabricator unknown

Waterfall and pond concept drawing

ing up bacteria if the water is not treated or sterilized. Sand particles are much smaller than bio-beads, and the particles trap dirt and debris which is held in the filter until it is backwashed out of the filter to a drain.

A sand filter works as dirt is collected in the filter, while the water flows through the valve at the top of the filter, and it is directed downward onto the top surface of the filter sand bed. The dirt is collected in the sand bed and the clean water flows through the lower piping at the bottom of the filter, up through the center pipe, into the control valve at the top of the filter. Clean water then returns through the piping system to the pool.

Please note that a sand filter removes suspended matter, and does not sanitize the water. The water must be sanitized with chemicals for clear, clean, potable water.

Canister Filters

Canister filters with replaceable cartridges are used primarily on small bodies of sterile water, such as a decorative indoor fountain. They work well only if there are not large amounts of algae, dirt, or debris, that can quickly clog the filter.

Purification System

Once you have chosen the proper filtration system for your needs, you can add the proper form of sanitation to the system. Sanitation is needed to kill harmful bacteria that can kill fish and harm humans, however, you must have the appropriate system for your specific application: biological versus sterile.

UV Sterilization

Ultraviolet sterilization is a proven, dependable and effective method for controlling and eradicating algae spores, bacteria and protozoa present in the water source without creating a toxic environment. Ultraviolet light alters or disrupts the DNA and RNA of target organisms. By properly implementing a disinfection system in-line, the targeted organisms can be eradicated effectively without any harmful residuals. This all makes it a good choice for ponds and water features that will contain fish or other aquatic life.

Chemical Sterilization

Chemical sterilization is used mainly to protect the public from disease. Chemicals such as chlorine and bromine are continually added to the water either through erosion devices or with electronic chemical injectors. These chemicals are added in small amounts sufficient enough to kill all micro-organisms. This sterilization is important if humans might have contact with the water, and run the risk of ingesting the water—even as residual water on a hand casually dipped in a fountain. Special chemical feeders are easy to install, and can be used with UV sterilization as a secondary level of safety. Of course no fish could survive in this system, but it is safe for humans.

Summary

Usually, a well balanced pond with sufficient aeration and plant life will stay very clear on its own. However, when life forms such as fish are introduced into the water feature, they become susceptible to disease, just as we humans are. To protect the aquatic life, we need some form of sterilization that won't harm it. You learned in this chapter that UV offers a great solution.

When building a water feature designed for humans, we need to be protected from diseases that can be found in water. We protect ourselves by chemically treating water that we will be ingesting or that we may come in close contact with.

Appropriate water treatment is really determined by the intended use of the water. Typically public fountains or publicly accessible water features would be regulated by your local health codes, and the proper guidelines ought to be followed.

Natural waterfall with sculpture, flowing into a swimming pool.

Trout aquarium and waterfall by
Rock and Water, Meramec Museum,
St. James, MO

Cascading waterfall into
swimming pool, Hong Kong
by Rock and Water Creations

Building
The Rock

Part   3

CHAPTER FOUR

The Rock Foundation

Concept drawing
for Grizzly
Industrial Tools
fountain,
Williamsport, PA

All sites vary a little in their requirements. Some sites will be indoors, while others may be outside in a backyard, or next to an existing swimming pool. The important aspect that all rock features will have in common, is the need for a solid foundation.

It is possible to build up a significant weight load when applying the cement to the rock structure; care should be taken to provide a sufficient footing to support the size of the final rock structure. Even when building on solid ground, you will want the rock to be supported by footers and secured to its site, in order to minimize the movement and settling that occurs—even on very hard ground. You may think that cracks in the mortar will look "natural" in your rock, but they

may also break watertight areas and create leaking, or doors may not close to pump rooms. A variety of problems can arise from a poorly supported structure, and it is difficult to anticipate things that could go wrong.

Preparing The Site

Regardless of the type of rock feature you are creating, you will need to do some site preparation. Site work can include: excavating for ponds, streams, plumbing trenches, electrical trenches, and support footers. If you are building on a pre-existing slab, you will need to drill anchor holes for rebar, or for anchoring the channel for the steel studs.

If your rock is small, you may be able to "get by" with rebar stakes driven into the ground. However, this is the least acceptable way of anchoring the structure and should only be used for small boulders.

After analyzing the different approaches to creating a structure in the following chapters, you will need to choose the method that will work best for you. Once you have made this decision you will know how to best anchor and support the structure. You will put the entire project at risk if you do not have an adequate base or foundation.

The Outline of the Rock Formation.

Use a garden hose or rope laid out on the ground to determine the size and shape of the rock structure. Mark the final shape on the ground with an aerosol-spray marking paint by painting the line of the hose. Also make sure to define any boulders which may be along the edge of the pond. You will first want to mark some measurement lines from your plan view drawing, so you will be able to "connect the dots" on the ground with a solid line, translating the scale drawing back onto the base or ground surface. Once the outline is complete to your satisfaction, mark the locations of the components to be included in the feature, such as the skimmer, drain, overflow, water level sensor, and jets.

Excavate Plumbing and Electrical Trenches.

If it is necessary to cross the water feature with plumbing or electrical conduit, make certain that trenches will be below the pond floor level. You can sometimes put the electrical conduit on top of the pond floor level, because you will be adding four inches of sand on top of it. It is always a good idea to keep as much of the plumbing and electrical service that is underground to the outside boundary of the pond or rock feature. If any underground component needs to be

Your geographic location will determine how deep to make the footer as they need to be below the frost level. The footer should follow the general outline of the rock formation and rebar stakes should be imbedded in the footer so the rock structure can be tied into the footer.

repaired in the future, it will be much easier to access it if it is outside the feature's structure.

Excavate the Pond and Footer

Once the plumbing is in place, you can excavate the pond and footer. Do not forget where you have plumbing buried, so as not to damage the pipes during excavation. If you buried your plumbing sufficiently below the lowest point of the pond, you will not have to worry about this.

Depending on the size of the rock water feature, you may need a footer that follows the outline of the artificial rock structure. The footer can follow the "lay of the land" but for any sizable structure, you ought to go at least below the frost level for the depth of the footer. Small boulders will not need a footer. However, a small footer that follows the edge of the boulder will be helpful in anchoring the rebar and holding it solid, while work is done on the boulder. For

small boulders, rebar stakes can be driven into the ground, spaced every ten inches along the outline of the boulder to hold the finished rock secure. Again, be careful not to drive a stake through the plumbing or electrical conduit. Boulders or structures with a footer will also have rebar stakes embedded in the footer every ten inches. These will later be used to connect the rock structure to it.

Where boulders overlap the pond edge, you will want the boulder to appear to be sitting naturally in its location, so the waterside of the boulder will be underwater, down to the bottom of the pond. A liner will be needed under the boulder, so "L" shape stakes ought to be installed in the concrete pond shell to define the waterside edge of the boulder. This way you will not pierce the liner under the shell by driving a stake through the liner. If you are not pouring a pond shell, you may want to secure each "L" shape stake in a mound of concrete, just to hold it as it sits on the liner. Once you are out of the pond with the rock outline

Concept drawing for Branson Horizons waterfall and koi pond, Branson, MO

Use the component checklist to make sure you have included all the necessary equipment before you begin making the rock.

The picture shows a 45mil liner over a smooth concrete shell. A sand base could be used in place of the concrete shell. Also notice the skimmer at the edge of the pond, always a good idea. We now prefer to use two drains with flanges that capture the liner, however the method pictured uses only one penetration of the liner minimizing your risk of a leak.

you can begin to drive straight stakes into the ground. Make certain you are not driving them through the water containment liner.

Lay In the Sand Bed

The sand bed will act as the transition from rough ground to a smooth soft surface for the underlayment and the liner. The liner will then be covered by rocks or a concrete pond shell. You should have, at a minimum, three inches of sand. The sand should be laid wherever the liner will be lying, and smoothed out to form a soft, even surface.

Installing the Plumbing and Electrical Housings

At this time, install all components that will be incorporated into the rock feature. This includes the suction drain, the skimmer, the overflow, the underwater j-boxes (if needed) for electrical service, and the water level sensor pipe, or equipment housing. When installing the different components, remember that you have 3 to 4 inches of sand, and then, on top of the sand you will have 3 to 4 inches of concrete. Suction drains and other elements must be set at the correct elevation, above the rough grade of the pond shell to allow for the addition of the

sand base and the concrete shell. You will want the drain to be located at the lowest finished grade of the pond for complete drainage during the emptying of the water feature, and also so that most debris will be pulled into the suction drain for filtration from the bottom of the pond. It is critical that the suction drain be at the correct elevation for the final layer of concrete, including any texture coats, such as a "pebbled" bottom. If you are not pouring a concrete pond shell, you can place the suction drain almost level with the final sand layer and attach the liner to the suction drain. You will want a suction drain made for this purpose, so it will have a water-tight flange for holding and compressing the liner around the edge of it.

When adding components to the pond, it is best to minimize the need to pass through the liner. Each conduit or pipe that penetrates the liner will need a water-tight flanged seal. It is crucial that these penetrations be done with a mechanical flange. Do not try to silicone the liner to the pipe, as it will not hold. If you have a leak, 99% of the time it will be at one of those locations that pierce the liner. In most cases, with the exception of the suction drain and skimmer, it is best to come up and over the edge of the liner, so there are fewer penetrations to the liner. However, this is rarely possible when installing skimmers and drains.

Waterproofing

The concrete shell and waterproofing is the foundation of the entire project. Without a good foundation, and sound water containment, the entire project is at risk. Your decision about which type of water proofing to use should be made with a combination of variables in mind: the quality of the material, the ease of installation, durability, the area to be waterproofed, and your budget. Typically, for most ponds, a 45-mil "fish-safe" EPDM rubber lining, with a durable underlayment, is the best choice. EPDM liner is flexible and easy to install. It is

also an economical choice. However, if you need to waterproof the sides of a vertical waterfall, you will need a barrier that will adhere to the concrete base and allow you to put the artificial rock layer on top of it. Liquid applied membranes work well for this.

There are several choices for liquid applied membranes, which include "elastomeric" coatings, and "cementitious" coatings, some of which incorporate an elastomer additive into the cementitious mixture. We have had the best luck with a purely elastomer form of coating. Some manufacturers claim that their products do not transfer any chemicals to the water, once it has cured. This is important if fish will be living in the pond.

Shown is a liquid applied membrane over a smooth concrete shell.
Sheraton Hotel, Sioux Falls, SD

Cementitious coatings need very strong bases to ensure against cracking, as it will not stretch or fill in over a crack. Cementitious waterproofing is used in the large aquariums that have 10" or more of steel-reinforced concrete as a base.

In chapter 5, we discuss the different types of structures and the most suitable waterproofing for each of them.

36

Summary

Most people who do not have much experience with construction, under-estimate the requirements for a foundation. Do not make the mistake of laying in a shallow footer or building the rock structure on a weak foundation. You will be devoting a lot of energy, time, and money to your project, and you will want it to last a lifetime. Excellent waterproofing is equally important; both a solid foundation and a waterproof liner are interdependent elements of a successful project. If the foundation moves, it may break the liner; if the liner leaks, it can weaken the ground around the foundation causing it to sink or fail. In both cases, it would be better to "over-do it" rather than to cut corners or proceed too quickly.

Aerial view of pond, waterfall, and stream. Waterproofing and rock structures for World Golf Hotel, St. Augustine, FL

CHAPTER FIVE

The Rock Structure

Several forms of reinforcing structures have evolved over the years, beginning with a free-form rebar grid structure, and evolving into a welded steel structure, with GFRC (Glass Fiber Reinforced Cement) precast rock panels, made from molds of actual rock faces. The panels are welded to the structure, using metal brackets embedded into the back of the GFRC panels. This is the most common system used today, however, the welded steel structure approach requires specialized skills, such as welding, as well as lifting equipment.

Also, a supply of precast panels is needed; for this reason it is the form of construction that is mostly utilized by professional rock companies. Precast panels can also be purchased from some suppliers listed in the "Resources" section of this volume. Or, you can attempt to make your own panels, which will be covered in chapter 5.

Rebar grid structure with spacers and lath on the inside of the form.

For a novice rock builder, or for the professional who doesn't want to work with large, heavy, precast panels, I will recommend some alternative methods that can produce results that are just as successful, with much less cost involved in the materials.

Rebar Free-form Structure

This first method of free-form rebar structure is probably the oldest method of creating a rock structure, used widely by zoos and theme parks for a number of years.

The rebar free-form method is time consuming, but it offers a great deal of flexibility and is probably the least expensive method, especially if you are supply-

ing the labor.

Rebar can be easily bent using a pair of rebar benders, as shown in the photograph on page 40. Bender bars, as they are commonly called, are typically custom made. You can have a welder fabricate a pair for a reasonable price. They take some practice to use, but after bending a few angles, you will get the hang of it.

The first step in this process is to create a grid form, with approximately 10 inch spacing between the lines of rebar. The grid form starts from the rebar stubs embedded in the ground, or in the footer. The grid defines the basic shape of the rock and at each place the rebar intersects, it is tied with rebar tie wire. I prefer using quick-ties which are short prefabricated 6" lengths of wire with a loop on each end. They can be bought

in bundles. The loops are grabbed by a special, but inexpensive, quick-tie tool, that quickly twists the wire around the rebar as you pull it a few times. The entire rock structure should be tied together and defined by the rebar grid.

For most rock features you can use a #3 rebar that is 3/8" thick. Once the grid is defined and you are happy with the way it looks, begin backing the structure.

Backing is required to give the cement plaster a "base" to hold on to, as well as to provide support for the plaster while it cures. Expanded metal lath is widely used for this purpose, giving the strongest base with a minimal amount of flexing. The holes in the lath provide excellent surface adhesion for the plaster or "Gunite," but if you use lath, try to get the soft lath that is easy to bend, since there are different grades of "stiffness." A plastic lath works great for this step and it will not cut you the way metal lath will. Wear gloves when working with metal lath, as it is razor sharp.

Plastic spacers can be added between the lath and the rebar to allow the cement to fully surround the rebar. The spacers are actually called "chairs," used to elevate rebar. They are made to snap onto the rebar and they should also be tied with a piece of tie wire to hold both the spacers and the lath secure. Take this step into account when selecting

Rebar cage used to build the structural shell for the pond and waterfall. Once a 3"-4" layer of concrete has been used to cover the rebar it is smoothed out wherever the a liner will be laid on it. The liner will then be sand-wiched between this layer and the textured rock layer.

a spacer, for it will define how thick the shell of the rock will be. You may not want more than a 3/4" spacer, depending on the strength the structure will require. It is not always necessary to use spacers, unless you are looking for a very strong structure. In many cases, the lath can be attached directly to the back, or inside, of the rebar form.

While working on a large job in a for-eign country, we were not able to obtain lath. But, with some resourceful ingenu-ity, we used burlap in place of the metal lath. This also made an excellent backing material, which was easy to use and inex-pensive. It will need to be covered with a

very thin coat of cement plaster. Once the fabric is stretched and tied to the inside of the rebar structure, the cement plaster coat will give it the rigidity needed to hold a heavy layer of grout or shot-crete that the cloth alone may not be able to support.

If you are fortunate enough to have a shotcrete or a gunite machine, which are machines used to spray cement mixtures, covering the structure with a good "structural coat" is a quick and relatively easy task. However, if you are applying the cement by hand, be prepared to "break into a sweat." You may want to call a gunite or shotcrete company and get a price for covering your structure with a good solid coat. Be prepared to pay several hundred dollars for the serv-ice. Get a bid, first. Once you have the structural coat applied, the following coats can be done much thinner and in smaller batches.

At this point you are ready to add a smooth coat of cement grout, (a portland cement and sand mixture) to all areas that will eventually contain water. This

Bender bars (tools) used to bend rebar into free form shapes.

Begin the steel stud method by building a sturdy structure that has a very general rock shape, mostly flat angled sections, built in varying thicknesses of layers. These layers represent the rock layers found in most formations. The layers can be built at and angle and do not have to be constructed horizontally as seen in the pictures. Styrofoam is then added to the structure to further define the rock surface.

smooth coat is critical; it must be continuous, smooth, without holes, and done with special care. The smooth coat will be covered by the waterproofing. Gaps, holes, and sharp wire protrusions will not work. Your waterproofing will be only as good as this layer allows it to be. Waterproofing will be covered in more depth in the following chapter.

Steel Stud Structure

Personally, this is my favorite form of construction. It is fast; materials are easily found; and most laborers can do a good job with a minimal amount of supervision. The steel studs are light weight and will go together easily, using self-tapping screws. Build the structure just as you would build a wall for a house, except in this case build it in the shape of a rock formation.

Steel stud construction is a fast and easy method of creating a structure. The material used for sheeting the structure will vary depending on whether the structure is indoors or exposed to the elements.

The steel studs are strong, when a solid "sheeting" is applied. Depending on the use and the weight, you may need some stronger supports in strategic areas.

The pictures on this page show plywood and MDF as the sheeting material, because this was an indoor waterfall. If we were creating an outdoor water feature that would be exposed to the elements, it would all need to be covered with waterproofing material or the sheeting material itself would need to be resistant to moisture. Although I have yet to use "exterior sheetrock" for this purpose, I think it would be an effective alternative, as would any rigid exterior grade sheeting.

Once the steel frame is constructed and the sheeting attached, you can start to build the rock formations, using styrofoam sheets that are cut to width with a table saw or a hand saw. "Hot knives" are also a great tool for cutting styrofoam. The knives cost about $100 and more, but

Poultry netting or chicken wire is used in 2-3 layers covering all the surface and anchored frequently in order to pull the wire tight to the surface, minimizing tenting of the wire.

since the styrofoam is not intended to be structural, we simply attach it to the support structure with a few screws.

Once the surface of the rock has been successfully defined by the styrofoam, it needs to be covered with 2-3 layers of poultry netting, commonly called chicken wire. The chicken wire should be securely fastened to the structural sheeting. Use large washers, or pre-cut circles of aluminum that are available at most building supply stores. The large washer, or flashing, is necessary so that the large holes in the chicken wire will not be able to pull off the fastener. Fasteners ought to be used everywhere the chicken wire is not fairly flat to the surface. The more "tented" areas of chicken wire you have, the more cement plaster it will take to cover them, or fill in. At a minimum, fasten the chicken wire every square foot. This solidly secures the wire and helps eliminate tenting.

Try to bend and shape the chicken wire so you have good, sharply defined edges around the styrofoam. You do not want to loose all the shapes you have created with the styrofoam, and for this reason the wire needs to fit snugly against all surfaces. Chances are there will be plenty of areas for the cement plaster to form around the wire, regardless of how snug you make it.

for any sizable job, it is well worth the initial expense as it will save much labor.

The styrofoam comes in sheets, usually 2'x8', at most home improvement stores. You can get it in 4'x8' sheets from certain suppliers. Styrofoam blocks can be bought measuring up to 4'x4'x8', and can be used without any other structure in some cases. The expense is very high, however, so I prefer to use it for building out ledges and variations in the surface of the general rock formation created by the structure. You can layer the sheets of styrofoam to create thicker areas and in this case,

Try to keep the chicken wire creased with sharp corners around the foam. Doing this will preserve as much of the shape as possible.

42

Finished waterfall built with steel stud method. Notice the fiber optically lit waterfalls. Twilite Nightclub, St. Robert, MO, by Rock and Water

Now that the chicken wire is up and fully covers all the surfaces, begin applying the scratch coat of cement plaster or Gunite mixture. Gunite is a dry cement and sand mixture pushed through a hose with air, and hydrated at the nozzle, with water. A "plaster pump" pumps wet cement plaster through the length of the hose and pressurized air is mixed with it at the nozzle, causing it to spray out. Both processes work well; however, the gunite creates a lot of dust, since some of the mixture becomes airborne. I prefer the plaster pump method, recognizing that both methods have their pros and cons. The down side of the plaster pump is that you must use or lose the mixture, if there is more than you actually need. The dry mixture method can be stopped and started without the worry of having the mixture set up prematurely.

We will cover this step in further detail in the next chapter.

Concrete or Welded Steel Structure

This method is generally used on substantial commercial jobs by professional rock builders, often companies who have the ability to create very large structures that need to be very strong. Many times, these structures have to pass local or state inspections, meeting strict building standards. That is not to say the work cannot be done by a person with little experience, given that person has welding skills and is able to do concrete form work.

With this technique of rock building, a cast concrete wall or support structure is made to conform to a very general shape of the rock and water feature design. The rock shape is further developed by building out a steel tube or angle-iron grid which will be used to support the cast rock panels, or covered with lath, a scratch coat, and finished with a hand stamped, carved finish.

A cast concrete wall or cinder-block wall is formed to the general shape of the rock water feature. Later steel grid work is attached to the wall, building out the rock formation even more. Next the pre-cast rock panels are arranged and attached to the steel structure by welding a steel stub on the back of the panels to the framework or by tying the panels to it with wire. The panels are later backfilled with concrete and the seams between the panels are textured and sculpted. Sioux Falls Sheraton Hotel construction, Sioux Falls, SD

Alternative Structures

If you do not have to satisfy the requirements of a building inspector, who might not allow an alternative method of construction, there are several easy structures that can be quickly built for very little money.

The first is a straw bale structure. Yes, straw bales, even if they will eventually rot away. They can be used to create the initial rock shape, then covered with chicken wire and a strong coat of cement grout. The chicken wire and cement "shell" is really what will give the rock structure the strength it will need for long durability.

The straw bales are easy to stack and they work well for creating a layered or "stepped rock formation." The bales are more than strong enough to support the cement, and the chicken wire can be attached to them with large home-made "bobby" pins that simply pin the chicken wire to the bales. As shown in the pic-

ture below, houses can be built using straw bales, so why not a rock formation.

Basically, anything that is strong and can be stacked, such as tires, rubble, steel cans, styrofoam, etc., can be covered with chicken wire, and coated with cement grout or "shotcrete."

Summary

Just as the general shape of the rock and water feature is determined by the underlying structure, it is also supported by that structure. As in building a house, the foundation and support structure are crucial to a successful project that will solidly stand on its own.

When building the structure based on your design, you ought to be able to get a good idea of what the rock feature will eventually look like once the structure is completed, as the structure will determine the major shapes of the finished rockwork.

There are many approaches to building a structure. Careful consideration should be given to the pros and cons of each method before deciding on which method to use. You may even decide to incorporate all the methods into the same rock and water feature.

Concept drawing for hot tub or fountain.

CHAPTER SIX
The Rock Surface

Concept drawing for zoo habitat.

The surface texturing is the final step in the construction process before you can begin to paint the rockwork. Just about every person you talk to, who has made a career making artificial rock, has their own techniques for achieving the desired "texture." Many techniques have been passed around from company to company over the years and, regardless of the techniques used, the bottom line is: if it looks good, use it.

One aspect of rock texturing that cannot be learned quickly has to do with having a feel for how rock naturally fractures and weathers. This can only be learned by observing closely a variety of natural rock formations. It may seem overwhelming at first to assess how much detail, complexity, and diversity there is in rock surfaces. However, you can simplify what the rock should look like by looking for the large general shapes first. Create those shapes with your structure; then, with styrofoam or other materials, create shapes that are more specific, beginning to define any layering the rock might have. Once these two steps are completed, achieving the texture of the surface is not difficult. We will see that there are many techniques used to create a credible artificial rock formation.

Using a cement plaster pump, the crew sprays on a scratch coat that covers most of the chicken wire and coats all the surface. Polyester fibers can be added to the plaster mixture for added strength and better adhesion surface for the next layer of plaster.

You can do this step by hand by troweling the plaster onto your structure and brooming its surface so the texture coat will adhere to it.

A liquid applied waterproofing membrane is applied to all vertical surfaces that will be splashed or have water running over them. This is a very important step and several coats should be applied to assure the area is watertight. The vertical waterproofing should overlap the liner in the pond area.

The Scratch Coat

The scratch coat can also be considered part of the structure because it is what will give added strength to the structure. We are discussing it in this chapter because it is the essential component of the eventual rock surface. The scratch coat combined with the texture coat and reinforcement will create the "structural shell" of the rock feature.

There are two processes for applying the scratch coat: machine applied, and hand applied. Since the scratch coat is really the "structural shell" of the rock, it should be strong and thick enough to provide sufficient support for the overall structure and for anyone climbing or sitting on the rock structure. A good solid coat of cement plaster, 1" to 3" thick, depending on the size of the structure, should be applied to all surfaces, creating an "unbroken shell" that is monolithic or continuous. Because this coat requires a lot of material to cover the surface, and because cement can be heavy and difficult to work with, you might consider having a professional shotcrete or gunite company spray the structural shell. If

this is not an option, either because of your budget, or because the rock project is small, doing it by hand is just as good—although a lot of labor. Of course, if you are planning to use precast panels which have a textured finish, this method will not apply. The proper method for installing cast panels is described in the precast GFRC panel section of this book on page 52.

When applying the scratch coat, make sure that all the chicken wire is well covered. It is acceptable if the wire pattern shows through, or if small voids are present. You do not want big "bubbles" of chick-

en wire that will need to be covered again by the texture coat, as it might get in the way of the final sculpting or even show through the final texture coat.

Waterproofing

The scratch coat will need to be smoothed out wherever the water needs to be contained. You may have laid down a liner for the basin of the water feature, but a liner will not work on the vertical sides of the waterfall. So, we need to use a "liquid applied membrane" that will adhere to the vertical sides. This layer needs to overlap the edge of the basin's waterproofing so the water will not run behind the pond liner. Do not make the mistake of thinking that the cement plaster will offer any waterproofing, as it will not. The liquid membrane should be applied to the sides of the water feature if they will be receiving any splash, or if the waterfall will be flowing over these vertical areas. A smooth surface will be needed so you can paint the liquid membrane onto it. This is a very important step, as any leaks will be very difficult to fix once the texture coat has been applied over this area. The surface should be smooth and free of holes and protrusions.

Once the area has been thoroughly waterproofed and the waterproofing has dried, splatter the waterproofed area with a thin coat of grout and let it cure. This will provide a rough surface on which the texture coat can adhere effectively.

The Texture Coat

The process of making artificial rock is mostly enjoyable, however, creating the final texture coat is really where the fun and satisfaction begins.

The texture of the rock surface is dependent on the type of rock you have chosen to build, and you will want to stay consistent in creating the appropriate texture. It is a good idea to have samples, or pictorial references, depicting the type of rock you have chosen to replicate. You can look at them while texturing and carving the final cement coat and achieve consistency in the look of the rock.

Several commonly used techniques exist for creating rock texture, and it may be that by the end of your project you will have developed some of your own techniques. The first method we will look at is the stamped texture, using a texture pad.

A section of the rock is painted with latex rubber for the first step in making a mold. On the right, a texture pad is being made from a fairly flat area of rock. Layers of latex and cheesecloth or burlap are built up, until the desired thickness is achieved.

The texture coat is applied over the scratch coat and smoothed out. The cement plaster surface is then rolled with a powder release and the texture pad is pressed into the still wet cement plaster, creating the rock surface texture.

Texture Pads

You may be saying to yourself that you do not own a texture pad and wondering what you might do. Well, there are three choices: one, make a texture pad; two, buy some texture pads; or three, use an alternate form of texture pad, such as crumpled up tin foil.

Making your own texture pads is a great project, and one you will probably want to repeat several times. It also forces you to look very closely at the rock surface, which is something you want to do before beginning the rock project.

Anyone can make a latex texture pad. All you need is some latex rubber (See Resources) and some cheese cloth or burlap. Begin by finding a good site which will allow you easy access to a large rock face or boulder. The site should be close by, and not require a lot of effort to get to, since you will be returning several times over a few days—a private location is the best. Any public property will require permission. I know from experience that the city or county offices will get numerous calls from "good samaritans" about a "lunatic" painting the rocks unless you have permission from whomever owns or controls the rock's location.

Begin by cleaning off the rock surface with a large brush or pressurized air. Using latex rubber or another flexible mold material, paint a rectangle on a fairly flat area of the actual rock face approximately 16" x 25". Paint the latex so it completely covers the inside of the rectangle. For this first coat, be careful to get the latex in all the "nooks and crannies." Let it sit until the latex is almost dry, but still just a little tacky. While that layer is drying, cut a bucket full of 6" to 10" square pieces of cheesecloth or burlap. Return to the site with the squares and coat the rectangle again with latex. As you coat the rock for the second time, lay a square piece of cloth on the rock and work it down into the cracks and shapes of the rock surface, adding more latex to the top of the cloth as you cover the entire rectangle with latex and cloth, allowing it to dry to a tacky surface between layers. This step can be completed as many times as you need to build up a thick layer of latex and cloth. When it is completely dry, this will become your texture pad. I like a pad that is about 1/4" thick as it gives the pad a "stiffness" that makes texturing on vertical sides easier.

Allow the pad to dry thoroughly, for several days, until all the "white" of the

The textured cement plaster surface is carved with cracks and fishers, while it is in a "cheesecake" like consistency.

Texturing the Final Coat

The texture pads you have made or purchased will be used to create and define the fine texture of the rock surface. However, wet cement plaster will stick to the texture pads if there is no "release" between the pad and the wet cement when the pad is pressed into it. A release agent, or mineral powder, is needed to keep the pad from sticking. Release powders are commercially available, (See Resources) and they come in a wide variety of colors, usually available from local concrete supply stores. The powders are typically used by concrete finishers for stamping pool decks and driveways. Since the powders come in several colors, you will want to choose a color that will work with the type of rock you are creating—some of the colored powder will become a permanent coloration of the rock surface.

Begin by applying a 1" to 2" thick layer of cement plaster to an area no larger than what can be textured and sculpted before the plaster sets up. You should have about a half hour before the plaster gets too stiff, depending on the ambient conditions. Apply the cement mixture on top of the scratch coat with a trowel and smooth it out to form the general shapes of the rock, defining the corners of ledges. Once you have a fairly smooth surface, begin to apply the texture. The texturing should be done while the plaster is still very wet. You will want to have a small roller for applying the powder release. Cover the roller with the powder and roll it onto the wet cement plaster surface, covering all the area to be textured. This is no time to take a break;

wet latex is gone. When you are confident that the latex is dry, all the way down to the rock surface, remove the pad from the rock surface. This sounds easy, but it will take some muscle. Do not give up, it should eventually pull off of the rock. Do not worry about ripping the latex, as it is extremely tough, especially if you have followed the process correctly.

You now have a texture pad. Congratulations. It is good to have several, and you might want to make a few more pads from different areas of the rock, such as the top of the rock, the side of the rock, the face of the rock, etc. This ensures a variety of samples for you to use in creating an authentic rock texture.

Molds of rock surfaces being prepared for the GFRC coating that will be applied to the latex mold surface. When the thin coating has cured it will create a hard shell with an exact reproduction of the actual rock surface, that can be used to create the artificial rock.

you should be working quickly to assure that the cement does not get too "stiff" before all the texturing can be accomplished.

Carving the Textured Area

Once the area on which you are working has been textured, begin to draw, with a pointed trowel, the lines and cracks of the rock. No need to try and sculpt the rock at this point if it is still very wet, as you want the cement plaster to be stiff, but not so hard that it will not flake away in natural looking pieces that resemble rock chips. The cement plaster will not flake like this until it has had some time to cure. You can cut or draw cracks in while it is still wet but let the cement reach this stiff point before beginning to sculpt. Once the plaster has reached the stiff point you can begin to "erode" the cracks by flaking out little areas along the cracks. You will also want to cut out or sharpen up any areas that appear to be drooping or "squashed" by the texture pad. Typically you will sharpen up all the definition left by the texture pad. Do not worry about loosing the texture of the

pad in those areas which you are re-defining, as you can use a dry brush, working over the cut surface, to regain some of the lost texture, or to blend it in with the texture of the pads. Try stippling the areas with the brush also. Stippling is a technique of "pounding" the points of brush or broom bristles into the surface, creating a "speckled" texture. You may even try a wire brush with large gauge wires for stippling. This can be made by cutting a stiff wire broom's head into

Precast rock panels used to create the most realistic rock formations. Panels are made of a Glass or polyester fiber reinforced cement mixture, sprayed into a mold taken from an actual rock section.

hand held pieces. Do a lot of experimenting with different methods for blending the carved areas into the textured areas. You may develop techniques of your own with experience.

Precast Rock Panels

To get nearly "perfect" rock, you have to use cast panels that are cast from molds of actual rock faces. You can come close to creating rock that is as good as that found in nature, using the techniques you have already learned. However, to get rock that is nearly perfect, you have to have molds of actual rock surfaces. We use the casts taken from these molds made from actual rock surfaces to give us the panels that we will use in creating a very realistic rock formation. (See chapter 9 for complete step-by-step)

Creating the Rock Molds

Molds are created in very much the same way as the texture pads were created, except the molds require one more step, which is creating a hard shell on the outside of the latex coatings. When removed, we have a general "hard shell"

Tin foil layer temporarily glued to the finished latex texture pad or mold on the rock. The tin foil will keep the hard shell from sticking to the latex mold so the two can be separated.

shape that will hold the texture pad to its original form of the rock face. This hard shell can be created with Fiberglas, or a spray-on urethane foam. (See Resources) The foam is great to use because it cures almost immediately and takes very little effort to make a shell. It does not offer the strength of Fiberglas, but it can be reinforced later with glass fiber and polyester resin (Fiberglas) if you want it to last for several casts. A layer of tin-foil is needed as a separator between the latex and the urethane shell or Fiberglas, so it will not stick to the latex. You want to be able to pull the shell off separately from the latex rubber, so we need a "release" of some sort between the two; a layer of foil works well for this. I usually spray the finished latex mold with spray glue while it is still on the rock surface. Then I stick a layer of foil to it so that all the latex surface is covered and there is no chance that the shell or "mother mold" as it is also called, will stick to it. Now you can spray on the urethane foam, which comes in portable kits. Spray a shell about 4" thick and wait for it to cure—about 15 minutes. Once the shell is hard, remove it. After taking off the shell, remove the latex mold from the

Pre-cast rock panels are tied or welded to the rock structure and then backfilled with the cement mixture. Later the seams will be filled in and textured, in order to blend the panels together.

Installing Precast Panels

Working with panels is like putting a puzzle together. You might have four or five molds. The cast panels from these molds can be used whole, or broken into smaller pieces, and even mixed up so that it is not obvious that you are repeating the same cast in several areas. As long as the layering or bedding of the original rock formation is all oriented at the same angle, it will be difficult to tell that the casts have been repeated. Once the seams have been finished, very few people will be able to notice the repetition.

rock and lay the mold back in the shell, with the molded rock "face up." Now you have a mold to use to create a cement rock panel.

The professionals use a gunite or plaster pump, and spray a cement mixture into the mold, using chopped glass strand built up in layers to create a very strong and relatively light rock shell. They also embed steel bar or angle iron into the back of the panel, so the panel can be welded to the steel structure. You do not have to do this if you are going to tie the panel to the structure with tie wire.

The casts are tied or welded to the rock structure that you have already created. If you are tying the casts to the structure, hang them so you can get some cement mixture behind them. This may require letting the top hang out farther than the bottom of the panel. If you are welding the panels to the structure, no backfilling will be necessary, as long as the panels are very strong. The "back-filled panel technique" will require that the structure have some backing, as we

Once the panels have been securely welded or cemented to the structure, the seams are filled in. The seams are textured and sculpted so they blend from one panel to the other.

described earlier, in order to hold the backfilling cement mixture in place. The panels are backfilled in order to "glue" or bond them to the structure. This is where a cement pump is effective, as you can spray the cement mixture behind the panels, achieving good adhesion. If the panels are welded to the structure, all you need to do is fill in the seams. Since with this process, there is no backing on the structure, such as lath or cloth, you may have to add some lath or backing between the seams. This is used to hold the mortar in the seams, preventing it from simply falling through to the interior void behind the cast panels when it is applied.

turing section, and carve it. When finished, the panel surfaces should blend together and appear as one rock. The color of the seams may be different than the surrounding panel material. However, if the textures are similar, they will appear to blend once the paint has been applied. What will not entirely disappear is the difference in the texture of the seams, if the seams do not have the same texture as the cast rock panels. For this reason take care to match the texture of the rock panels as closely as possible.

The entire rock structure is pressure washed, removing all the release powder and cement carving debris. The surface must be clean and free of loose material for painting.

Blending the Seams

Once all the panels are "in place" and permanently attached to the structure, either by cementing them or welding them on, the work on the seams can begin. The seams should be filled so they are just a little raised above the panel level. This will allow enough material to carve, and "blend" the panel surfaces together.

First, smooth out the seam area and try to blend the panels in a very general way, extending ledges and grooves. Texture the area, as described in the tex-

Stressing and Cleaning the Finished Surface

The last steps to accomplish before painting the rock are stressing and pressure washing the surface. When cast panels are used, you need to break or chip (with a hammer) some of the areas along the panels' edges that will reveal them to be cast panels. In other areas of the panel seams, you may need to hand-patch those sections that do not look textured or carved. Places along the panel edge, that may have been broken off, will also need some attention.

Once hand patching and chipping are finished, pressure washing the entire structure, being careful to wash off all of the release powder used for texturing, is the next step. If this powder is not removed, the paint will not adhere to the surface of the rock. A good pressure washing job should get all the powder and debris off the rockwork.

Trout aquarium progress shot. Panels are hung on free-form, rebar structure, with burlap backing. Notice how panels are hung with wire. After panels are grouted in place the wires are cut and removed. Photo of finished aquarium on page 29.

cated rock surface that will require much less cost and effort than either making the panels yourself or purchasing precast panels. Using precast panels, however, allows you to create rockwork without requiring a great deal of sculpting skills.

Chipping and stressing the surface once it is cured hard can also help to disguise or blend areas that are not "rock like" in appearance. Hard cement mortar will chip and break in the same way that real rock chips and breaks. Wear safety

glasses and be prepared to work the muscles of your arms. It is a lot of work to create texture once the cement mortar has cured "hard."

Regardless of the methods used in creating the texture of the rock surface, the surface needs to be well cleaned before paint is applied. This can be done by pressure washing the entire rock feature from the top down.

The rock structure is very important, but it is the quality of the rock texture that will determine whether or not the rockwork is believable. Work conservatively until you have mastered the techniques you prefer to use in creating the rock surface.

Summary

There is a variety of techniques to use to create rock texture. Even crumpled up tin foil pressed into soft mortar can be used to create a rock texture. You will want to experiment with the techniques described in this chapter as well as develop some of your own.

Precast panels will give the most realistic looking rock if the budget allows for it. By using texture pads made from real rock and some hand sculpting, you can create a nice looking indirect fabri-

CHAPTER SEVEN

Painting The Rock

Fountain or spa concept drawing.

Different types of rock vary widely in color, ranging from light grey, to dark brown, reddish brown, golden yellow, or even pink. The color can vary widely among the same types of rock as well.

Most sedimentary formations have variations of similar color in each of the layers. Granite, an igneous rock, is found in a multitude of colors, depending on the minerals that were present when it was formed. Granite will typically be speckled with a "salt and pepper" appearance including flecks of color combined with white or pink crystals. In contrast, sedimentary rock, which has more blended areas of color, can have some banding or layering. Typically rocks are found with a combination of several colors, with a dominant color, and lighter or darker variations of that dominant color. Some formations can also have a

high content of iron, causing it to leach bright brownish red stains in certain areas. Native rock may also be aged, weathered, and darkened by algae, possibly appearing black or very dark brown.

The Rock Coloration

You will want to choose a few small, real rocks of the same type, for use in matching their colors to your artificial rock feature. The sample rocks should be small enough to take to a paint store for color matching. If you plan to include real boulders along the side, or as accents to your artificial rock feature, it would be a good idea to install them before you paint the artificial rock formation, so you can match the colors. You may also want some photographs of the real boulders you chose for selecting the matching paint. Having clear photographs of real rock with detailed close up views is necessary to get the color palette correct.

You will want to decide what the dominant color of the rock will be: brown, red, tan, or grey, for example. Once this is determined you can get three or four variations of this color, beginning with the lightest shade and ranging to the darkest shade. You will want some black, regardless of the color you chose, as well as some reddish brown, and possibly some orange or yellow. A flat exterior latex paint works very well for all colors.

Rock Painting Techniques

Begin with the lightest color as your "base" coat or the first coat of paint. Add enough water to the paint to create a milk like consistency and strain the mixture into a hand-pump style garden sprayer. Completely coat all surfaces with this base coat. The paint should be thick enough to coat the rock but thin enough to pass through the garden sprayer. Be careful to coat all surfaces, including any underside of ledges.

For the next coat, mix up the next darkest shade of your color range. You can apply this coat while the base coat is still wet and the two will blend together. Do not cover the entire surface with this coat. Leave some areas of the initial coat showing through. You will repeat this process for each of

the three or four shades you have chosen to use. Save the reddish brown and black for the final steps. Each coat of the three or four different shades should be applied so as not to cover completely the previous shades. This will give a "variegated" color pattern. Apply the different colors so there are not a lot of hard edges between the colors. For example, we do not want a "military camouflage look," with large patches of sharply defined spots, but rather the colors should all blend, creating soft transitions between neighboring colors. These first three or four colors will all need to be painted while the previous coats are still wet, in order to achieve this effect.

If you are painting a granite rock, you

A base color is sprayed on to the rock surface being careful to cover all areas.

will want to use the same pressure garden sprayer to apply the base coats in the way previously described. However, some granite has a speckled look which requires a slightly different approach. The effect can be achieved with the same garden sprayer but the base coats will need to be dry, so the speckled colors will not blend into the other base colors. Choose which colors will be used to create the speckles, and using the sprayer

to apply the color, adjust the sprayer to a mist or light spray; this way the color goes on very lightly and "speckles" the rock surface when sprayed. This will give the desired "salt and pepper" or "speckled" look that is characteristic of granite.

For a sedimentary rock formation you can paint, with a brush, the different shades of banding or layers of the rock, as seen in the photos on this and the previous page. Be careful to keep the shades of the rock layers within the borders of the appropriate layers. The layers should have been defined by a fracture line carved into the cement during the carving process. Once all layers of color, shade variations, or speckling is complete, and all the coats of paint are dry, one can begin to paint the black and rust colors that help to define the relief of the rock texture and give the rock an "aged" look.

Finished painted rock surface in the style of pink quartzite.

The other colors are painted on top of base coat. Being a sedimentary type of formation, different shades were painted in each of the layers. The layers were defined during sculpting by cutting a line in the wet grout after it had been textured.

Black is injected into the cracks and then sprinkled with clean water so the black paint will spread out and look like natural stains.

A good tool to use for "aging" the rock is a large syringe. One type of syringe is typically used for injecting meats with spices. These syringes can be found at most grocery stores. Also, veterinary suppliers have large animal syringes that work well. The syringe is used to "inject" the watered down black paint into the cracks and crevices. Again, the paint should be the consistency of milk. Have the black paint in a small bucket and draw the paint into the syringe. Have the garden pressure sprayer full of clean water, ready for use. Inject some of the black paint into a crack, dragging the syringe along the crack while dispensing black paint with slow constant pressure on the syringe. After the syringe has been emptied, lightly "spritz" the black paint with clean water. The key is to get all the runs and drips of black paint to spread out with the water so that you do not have ugly drip lines. It should all look like areas of natural rock that have darkened due to mineral deposits and water seepage from

the rock crevices, for example. It may take some practice to get just the right amount of water, so you do not wash away all the black.

On the other hand, you do not want solid, dark lines from the dripping black paint. The black paint ought to be all "feathered out" by spraying it with clean water while the black paint is wet. Start with major fracture lines and some of the smaller cracks, but leave some areas without black. This is where design and aesthetic decisions will need to be made; you do not want too much black but too little may not look

good either. Some areas should be more "solidly" covered while other areas will have less black. The goal is to avoid a "uniform" look. Try practicing on a hidden or obscured area of the formation first until you decide how much is the appropriate amount of black for the look you want. You can always add more of the black, but you do not want to hide all the base colors you have previously applied with too much black paint.

The last colors to be used are rusty red colors and bright yellow or gold colors. These should be used very sparingly; just a few areas should be "washed" with these bright colors. These bright colors are applied in the same way as the black. Apply the watered down rust or gold color either with the sprayer or the syringe, and then sprinkle the paint with a little water in order to feather out the paint.

Summary

Find an area of local native rock with the coloration you like and try to match three or four of the major colors in the rock. These colors will become the base colors used for the first few coats. Work from the lightest color to the darkest color and do not attempt too much detail too quickly. Paint large broad areas, mixing different shades, and blending them on the rock surface. The base coat is the "under" painting of the rock. The black and rust staining is put on after the base coat darkens and this will give the rock "life." If you are not happy with the final product simply apply the base coat to the rock again and start over. Try not to be intimidated by the painting process as it ought to be fun, creative, and one that requires little technical skill, if the right colors have been chosen and the steps outlined are followed.

Rock waterfall and spa for a themed hotel room in Reno, NV. Notice the use of murals to expand the illusion of the rock and create a tropical ocean paradise. The spa was plumbed so the return water created a waterfall back into the spa. A life size model of a sea otter was placed on the rock to further enhance the realistic experience. Rock by Larson Co. Mural by J. Erik Kinkade

The color swatches at the bottom of each picture represent the suggested base colors for getting the color of the rock in the photo. You may still need to have black, and some rust color for staining effects.

Cascading waterfall into swimming pool, Chatsworth, CA by Rock and Water Creations

Step-By-Step
Guide

Part 4

CHAPTER EIGHT

Step-By-Step
Hand Textured Technique

The following is a step-by-step, complete process of constructing a medium sized artificial rock project for a backyard waterfall using the standard frame method with hand texturing.

1 Draw the outline of the rock feature

Lay a garden hose on the ground where the outline of the rock formation will be. Play with different shapes and sizes until you are satisfied with it. Using a can of aerosol marking paint, paint the outline of the hose so you have a permanent line to use as a guide.

You should also be considering how you will plumb the waterfall, as you may need to bury pipes at this time too.

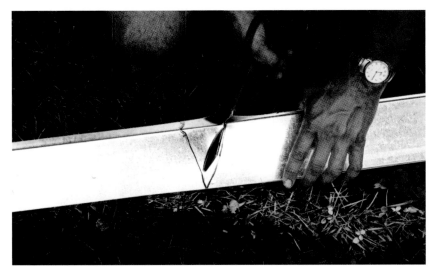

We chose to use tin or metal framing studs and track to construct this waterfall. Pressure treated studs can also be used. However, metal studs are easily cut, light weight, and will not rust. Once the sheeting is applied, it makes a very strong structure.

Metal track is slightly wider than metal studs and the track is used to hold the metal studs. The studs will fit inside the track and may be screwed to it with self-tapping screws. Metal framing is available in different gauges and the lightest gauge is the easiest to use because it cuts easily.

By making a straight or angled cut through one side and the bottom of the track, you can make bends in it. You will eventually need a metal stud at each bend, so do not make an excessive amount of bends. The goal is to follow the outline of the rock formation with the track. Straight lengths of track are used, placing bends wherever the outline has a major change in its direction.

Once the track has been cut and formed to the outline on the ground, drive 8" spikes through the track into the ground, securing it. If the rock feature is large and the ground is soft, you may want to pour a concrete footer and attach the track, or pressure treated studs, to the footer.

3 Cut and place studs for wall

Many of you are familiar with topographic maps. Your structure is similar to a topographic map in three dimensions. That is to say each layer of the rock is formed as a "tiered" structure, like a wedding cake, only in the shape of a rock.

First, decide how high to make the first layer. You may need to vary the heights of the sides to compensate for a slope or unevenness in the ground. Using metal studs, not track, cut as many studs as you will need to form the walls of the first layer. A power cut-off saw with a metal cutting blade will make the job much easier and faster than trying to cut each one by hand.

It is possible to create a rock form without building in layers by building a "tent" type of structure. However, for this demonstration we are creating a "layered" form of rock formation.

Using self-tapping screws, attach the studs to the track by placing a screw at the joint where the track overlaps the stud. Screw from the outside of the track on both sides. You may need to hold the two layers of steel together with a pair of pliers while another person puts in the screws. Typically the screws will go in without a lot of difficulty.

Make sure to place a stud at each bend in the direction of the track. We will need a stud at this location so that

we will have something to attach the plywood sheeting to. Space out the other studs, each one at an average of 12" to 16" apart.

4 Form the top track

When all the studs are in place and secured to the bottom track, begin to form the top of the wall. The top of the wall is formed with the same track material used on the bottom of the wall. By cutting a line through all but one side of the track you can form it around the top, just as you did the bottom. It may work best to secure the track to the studs as you go. This will allow you to get the bends and cuts in the proper location. The top track is basically just a mirror image of the bottom track.

If using metal studs and track, make sure to wear gloves whenever possible as the track material is sharp and can easily cut you.

5   Place the cross pieces

Lay studs across the structure to support the next layer. The cross members should be strong enough to support a person walking on the surface. You can see in the photograph, an interior wall was needed to shorten the span of the cross members. The cross members are stronger if they are used on edge. However, it was easier to lay them flat on our structure, and since this was a small structure, we felt it would be enough support. Also, since we are adding several layers, each layer will add even more strength to the structure.

Cover the first layer with plywood

Once the structure has been built, cover it with, preferably, pressure treated plywood, 3/4" thick. The plywood will make the structure very strong and should be screwed to the metal studs every 12" to 16". Use either a drywall screw or self-tapping metal screw. The screw ought to be long enough to go through the plywood and approximately 1/4" into the metal stud. If the structure is made of pressure treated studs, use drywall screws long enough to go through the plywood and, at a minimum, 1/2" into the stud. Make sure to mark where the studs and cross members are located under the plywood so that once they are covered, you will know where to put the screws.

On the sides of the framework, you should have a joint at each change of angle. Now you see why we needed a stud at each of these locations. We needed someplace to secure the ends of each side piece of plywood. This is where the neighboring pieces butt-up to each other. You will need either stud at this point, or two studs on either side of the angle change.

Although good carpentry skills are an advantage, the entire structure will be covered with a layer of grout, so you do not need to be overly concerned with making precise cuts, as long as you do not have big gaps or extending edges.

Always use safety glasses and proper safety equipment when working with power tools.

7 Form the walls for the second layer

Using a hose, lay out the general shape of the second layer of the rock. This is done just as we did previously for the first layer. The hose will be curved; however, we translate the curves into short straight lines for the track that will be laid on the surface of the first layer. The track is cut and shaped in the same way we laid the track for the first layer. Instead of using spikes to secure it, we will use drywall screws, fastened into the top of the first layer.

We wanted to plan a bench area for sitting and so the second layer of the rock was set back, creating a comfortable space for two or three people to sit. The next level of the rock will act as the backrest. I would avoid having too many big over-hangs, as it is difficult to get the grout to cover the underside of the over-hang. The second layer and the following layers should be designed so they do not follow the shape of the preceding shapes. This will give a more varied and natural look to the waterfall—each layer of the rock having a unique shape.

Complete all the following layers

If you are building an artificial waterfall, you will want to consider where the water will flow and how that waterflow would have naturally changed the real rock. In a natural waterfall, the water will have eroded the rock, creating curved shaped "set-backs" in each of the layers over which the water flows. You will also need to consider how level the rock is, and how the water will flow over the finished rock. You will want the water to flow over the preferred side of the rock, and so you may have to compensate for a slope in the natural terrain or grade on which the rock feature is sitting, making some sides taller than other sides, creating a more level plain for directing the flow of the water. Edges can be built up in the next step to help direct the flow of the water. However, any compensation for uneven ground, over four inches, should probably be accomplished with the support structure.

Our first layer needed to have one side that was 14" tall and the oppos-

ing side 8" tall in order to achieve a more level rock formation. We made the walls of the first layer gradually slope, to create a more level surface. This meant cutting each stud in the first layer at a custom length. The second layer was then made with the same lengths of studs for all the walls, and covered with plywood. The same procedure was followed for each of the succeeding layers.

It is recommended, although not shown, to cover the wood structure with tar paper before proceeding to the next step in order to prevent water seepage from damaging the structure later on.

9 Cut polystyrene foam pieces

Polystyrene foam, commonly known as Styrofoam, is characterized by the white "bead" construction seen in a coffee cup. It is available in sheets at most home building stores. The foam is cut in strips and used to define the ledges and layering of the rock. The layering defined by the foam pieces should be consistent in the width of each layer as you go around the larger layers of the structure. Imagine each layer of sediment that was laid down to create native rock. Each layer will be roughly the same thickness and "at the same level" all the way around the rock. Just as the layers of the

structure that we built out of metal and wood are the large general layers of rock, the foam defines smaller layers of the structure within these larger layers.

The foam will be what gives the rock its characteristic shape. Since the foam is not a structural element of the rock, it only needs to be "tacked" on to the structure with a nail or drywall screw. Make sure you use the foam on the top surfaces to direct the desired flow of the water. You will also want to consider forming the foam around the pipes that will supply the waterfall.

Cover the structure with chicken wire

Unroll a length of chicken wire long enough to be folded into two layers. The length should be enough to go completely around the rock formation. The width of the chicken wire is not essential, a wider roll may save you some time, depending on the size of your structure. A metal washer with a drywall screw through the middle of it, will be used for anchoring the wire to the structure. You will want to use a metal washer, 1 1/4" or larger, so the washer cannot pass through the holes of the chicken wire. The washer needs to have a center hole small enough that a drywall screw will not pass through it. You can also use flashing material cut into squares as an alternative to the washers. The chicken wire should be anchored so that it conforms tightly to all areas of the structure. Care ought to be taken to ensure that the chicken wire does not "tent" around the foam pieces. This will require putting anchors close to the foam pieces and possibly pounding the wire into shape, so it fits tightly around the shapes of the foam.

The entire surface will need to be covered with the two layers of wire so the cement scratch coat will have a reinforcing surface to adhere to. Be liberal with the use of anchors, and at a minimum, anchor it at every 16" square. Do not worry about areas where the wire overlaps more than two layers, as too many layers of wire is not a problem. However, uncovered areas should be avoided.

11 Coat the structure with a scratch coat

Use "one" 90 lb. bag of portland cement, mixed with "three" 50 lb. bags of "play sand" or mason's sand for each batch of "mortar." The consistency of the mixture should be similar to that of sour cream, or soft butter. The goal is to have it sticky, yet wet enough to stay on a vertical surface and be easily spread or troweled.

Completely coat all the surfaces with 1/2" to 1" thick mortar, taking special care to cover the underside of any protruding ledges. The chicken wire should be completely covered by this coat; however, it is acceptable to have some of the chicken wire pattern show through at this stage. Any areas that will need to

hold water, or that will be hit by splashing, will need to be troweled smooth in preparation for waterproofing. All other surfaces should be roughed up slightly by dragging a bristle brush or broom over the surface. This will give the final texture coat a rough surface for better adhesion.

It is easiest, when applying the mortar mix, to have a pallet specifically called a "truck" by brick masons, which is used for holding a mound of the mortar. With the other hand, a "pool" trowel is used to sweep the mortar off the truck and onto the wall, while holding the truck up close to the wall. If you are not familiar with this, ask your local home store for a simple demonstration of their usage. Once you get the hang of it, it will go quickly without a great deal of effort. It may be necessary, however, to "throw" small amounts of the mortar into areas that are difficult to get your tools into. Just be careful not to lose the shapes of the foam pieces. Try to maintain crisp corners on all the foam shapes you have applied to the structure.

Paint on the waterproofing

When the scratch coat has cured and is dried, you are ready to begin waterproofing. All areas that will hold or come in contact with the water will need to be waterproofed with a minimum of two coats of a liquid applied waterproofing membrane. (See Resources) These areas need to have been smoothed out during the previous step. This will eliminate any sharp edges or wire protrusions that might exist to compromise the waterproofing. The waterproofed area needs to be clean and free of debris before applying the waterproofing. The cement mortar will not offer any waterproofing if left untreated, and extreme care ought to be given to this step, as any future leaks will be very difficult to fix once the texture coat has been applied. You may wish to do a water test once the waterproofing is completed to check for any possible leaks. It is well worth any extra time or effort at this stage to prevent or discover a leak that would otherwise be covered by the texture coat.

13 Apply the texture coat

Before applying the texture coat, moisten the cured and dried scratch coat with a mist of water. This will help the texture coat adhere to the scratch coat. The texture coat gets applied in the same fashion as the scratch coat, in an approximately 1" thick layer. Work on an area small enough so that it can be textured before it begins to cure and get stiff. This may only be an area that is as big as your texture pad. You will eventually be able to do larger areas when you become familiar with the process and are better able to work fast. First, smooth out the mortared area so most of the trowel marks are gone and you have a smooth surface. Take care to define corners of protruding ledges and other shapes created by the original foam forms we applied to the structure. Completely coat all surfaces of the area to be textured. This may include bottoms of protruding ledges and tops of the ledges.

The best texture pattern will be achieved if it is done while the cement is very "green" or wet. The scratch coat beneath the textured coat will draw much of the moisture from the texture coat, which will rapidly make it unworkable. Quickly move on to the next step to apply the release powder.

Apply the release powder

Next, with a small paint roller coated with release powder, slowly roll the entire area of wet cement, applying a thin coat of release powder over the surface. Continue to dip the roller into the pail of release powder, replenishing the roller's supply of powder, so that all areas get a good, even coat. You only want the release powder on the wet cement area that has been troweled smooth and will be textured. Be careful not to get the release powder on uncovered areas of the scratch coat. For this reason, you will want to work from the bottom of the rock feature up to the top. This will help to prevent the release powder from falling onto, or otherwise getting onto untextured areas of the scratch coat. If the release powder does get on unworked areas of the scratch

coat, it will prevent the cement mortar, of the texture coat, from adhering to it. Avoid breathing the release powder by wearing a dust mask.

Once you have coated the wet cement mortar with powder, you are ready for the next step, which is texturing.

15 Texture with the press pads

and one that is used for the tops of the rock, as these two textures will differ in their texture. If you do not have a texture pad, and you do not want to make them or purchase them, you can try using crumpled up tin foil. Believe it or not, the crumpled tin foil, when unfolded, will have a convincing texture similar to many kinds of rock. The foil is used just as you would use the texture pad.

When the area to be textured is completely covered with a thin layer of powder, hold the texture pad up to that area, making certain that any layering defined on the texture pad is oriented to follow the layering of the rock feature you are creating. While holding the pad steady, press it into the wet cement. Use the palm of your hand and press all areas of the pad, without moving the pad's location, so that the entire area covered by the pad gets textured. It is always a good idea to have a texture pad that will be used for the vertical sides of the rock,

Once all areas have been textured, using a small trowel, cut cracks or fracture lines into the wet cement. Before the cement gets completely hard, you will want to carve or chip the crack lines to create a more realistic looking crack. Do not let the cement get too hard before this is done. You may have to carve a textured area before going on to another area for texturing. There is a point in the curing of the cement, when it is wet enough to flake off, and dry enough to flake off in natural chip-like pieces. This is the optimum time to carve it.

Clean the surface

Now that the entire rock has been textured and carved, we need to remove all of the release powder and carving debris. In order for the paint to adhere well and be absorbed into the cement, we will have to have a surface free of debris and release powder.

A pressure washer is the best tool for cleaning the surface. Usually a household garden hose will not have adequate pressure to remove all of the release powder, but if you do not have access to a pressure washer, scrub the surface with a brush, and wash it off with a hose and sprayer attachment. The release powder must be thoroughly removed from the surface.

Working from the top of the rock feature down to the bottom, hit all surfaces with the power washer, making sure to expose a clean cement surface. When the rock is clean, let it dry before beginning the next step. You may need to broom or vacuum the puddles of water off the surface, to speed up the drying time.

17 Select the rock colors

Before beginning to paint, decide what colors to paint your rock. If there are any real rock formations in your area, you may want to use them as a guide in choosing the colors to be used. You will need three or four colors for the base coat. These are the colors that will define the overall color of the rock. For our

Do not be too concerned with choosing exactly the right colors. You will be able to mix different combinations of the colors you have chosen in order to get a wide variety of colors. All the mixed colors will have a similarity, since they were mixed using different amounts of three or four base colors.

rock project we selected the colors illustrated in the color swatches on this page. The rust color and the black are used as highlights, while the first four colors were used as the base colors.

Rock varies widely in coloration, so the only guideline to follow is to choose a range of values. Value is the darkness or lightness of the color. For example, if you were able to see the colors in black and white, you would want colors that ranged from light gray to a dark gray or black. You can see this in a black and white photograph. The swatches above are laid out from the lightest value to the darkest value.

You will want a good grade of exterior latex paint with a flat finish. If you can find a paint made specifically for stucco, this would be a good choice, but not necessary. The stucco paint is more resistant to the alkalis in the cement. However a standard latex house paint will last many years and the rockwork may never need to be repainted. The only noticeable difference you may see with time is some fading of color. The bright reds and yellows will be the first to fade, but most of the rock colors, such as brown, gray, and tan, will show very little fading over time. Since the paint is absorbed by the cement, it will last nearly as long as the cement will last. You will not need to use any sealants on the finished rock as the paint will be sufficient to seal the surface.

Spray on the lightest base color

Start with the lightest shade of your base colors. Thin the latex exterior flat paint with water until you have a "milk" like consistency. The paint should be thick enough to coat the rock yet thin enough to be able to be sprayed through a garden type of pressure sprayer. You may need to strain the paint with a paint strainer so it will not clog the garden sprayer. This may seem like a primitive way of painting, however, the garden sprayer allows you to move freely around the rock while painting, and it also allows you to achieve different textures, like speckling. It also allows you to drench the surface with paint so that all the areas of the rock absorb some of the color. You will, however, need to clean out the sprayer frequently to avoid clogs.

Completely coat all surfaces of the rock with the lightest base color. Make sure to coat everything, including the underside of any ledges. Apply a generous amount of paint so it will run and seep into all the cracks and crevices. The intention is to stain the entire cement surface with the watered down latex.

Make a mixture of the next darkest color and spray areas of the rock with it, leaving areas of the first layer showing through. This can be done while the first coat is still wet, and they will blend together nicely. Repeat this process for each of the colors except for the rust color and the black color. The goal is to let some of each of the base colors show through. You may want to paint smaller and smaller areas as you apply each of the base colors. Subtle transitions, from one color to the other, will make the best looking base. This will happen naturally if the paint is applied while the previous coat is still wet. You do not want to have a "camouflage" look where each color used has crisply defined edges creating a "patchwork" look.

When you are satisfied with the base coat coloration, let it completely dry before continuing to the next step. If you are impatient, you will find that a leaf blower, blown on the wet paint surface, not only helps dry it, but creates some interesting effects by blending the wet areas of paint into one another. As with most of rock making, experimentation with different effects can lead to some creative discoveries.

Inject black paint in the cracks

Obtaining a large syringe, such as those used for injecting meats with spices, or a horse vaccination syringe, fill the syringe with a watered down, pure black, paint. With a steady pressure on the syringe plunger, drag it along a crack or crevice while injecting the black paint into it. The paint will begin to run out of the crack— which is the effect we want. You do not want to paint all cracks and crevices. Leave some areas without the black. The major dividing cracks between layers of the formation are a good place to start, and then add some of the smaller cracks. Try not to have a "sameness" of black staining on the rock. That is to say, you want some areas to have more black staining than other areas. Do a small area with a single syringe full of black paint and then proceed to the following step. Repeat these two steps until you have the desired "look" of the rock. Be aware that the black paint will dry much lighter than the wet paint. You may need to go back over some areas, after the paint has dried, in order to achieve the desired effect.

While the injected black paint is still wet, mist it with just enough clean water so that the black paint spreads out on the surface. The most important part of this step is in not leaving any drips or runs that have not been "feathered out" by the water. The goal ought to be to create a weathered or stained appearance. Any hard lined drips or spots will simply look like drips of black paint, and will be difficult to cover up or eliminate, once the black paint has dried. For this reason the water should be applied immediately after the black paint has been injected into the cracks.

Congratulation! You should now have a finished artificial rock waterfall, enjoy.

CHAPTER NINE
Building Techniques Using (GFRC) Cast Rock Panels

Introduction by Rodger Embury

Retaining wall waterfall flowing into spa, concept drawing.

Some may disagree with me, but I don't see faux rockwork as a "sculptor's art form." For more than 25 years, I've made sure that Mother Nature is the one who does the detail work; what I do is take copies of her artwork to job sites and install them in creative and interesting ways.

A long time ago, I developed a method of making castings of real rocks using my own formulation of fiberglass and epoxy. These are exact replicas of the real thing: Once mounted on steel structures in swimming pools or other hardscape applications, the panels are blended together to

Roger Emery, founder of Rock and Water Creations, is a pioneer in the field of cast rock panels. Many of the techniques standard to the field were developed by Emery and his company.

make artificial rock formations that take full advantage of Mother Nature's eye for detail and texture.

I don't mean any disrespect to people who make their faux rocks on site and acknowledge the fact that trying to recreate with your hands what nature does through the eons is no small feat. But I also say without hesitation that using rock castings is the only sure-fire way to make certain the work looks real each and every time.

Taking It Easy

For 20 years, our firm used this technology strictly for our own projects. We've installed rockwork on pools and other watershapes throughout the United States and around the world using our inventory of rock panels -- and we've done it in an endless array of combinations and configurations.

These days, we still do a good bit of rock design and installation work, but we've also made the panels available to contractors for use in their projects. Although this is a relatively new direction for our business, so far the people who have adopted our method are having success with it -- and say they enjoy skipping the labor-intensive processes involved with creating their own faux-rock formations from scratch.

The best thing about what we do is that it starts with nature: The rocks are

selected in the field and come in an array of surprising shapes with fascinating contours, cracks and crevices, and the process of finding these specimens often sends me hiking through the hills and canyons of California and elsewhere searching for interesting rocks and formations to copy.

When I find something that catches my eye, I bring in my crew and make an impression of the rock structure. This means more than individual boulders or stones: we're after whole rock structures, not just isolated shapes. Back at our shop, we use these molds to create exact replicas of the originals. Once on site, we bring in finishers who color and do the final texturing on the panels to ensure their realistic appearance.

It's a neat process, but the best of it is that when we step on the job site, the hardest part is done. All that's left at that point is the installation and finishing, which is what this step-by-step pictorial is all about.

After selecting and purchasing your rock panels, they are loaded on a truck for transportaion to your job-site.

General Steps for Creating a GFRC Rock Feature

The first step is to design the rock feature in scale so you can determine the amount of square feet of rock panel you will need for the project. Rock panels are sold by the square foot, however just as a piece of paper is smaller after it has been creased and wrinkled it still has the same surface area as it did when it was flat. The same is true of rock panels with their shelves and uneven surfaces. Once you decide what the flat square footage is of your project including all sides and tops you should add approximately 30% to the figure in order to determine the actual square footage.

In order to support the weight of the rockwork, we preplan and design steel support into it. Backfilling the panels with concrete ensures a stable, long-lasting structure.

In the case of a residential swimming pool installation, for example, the bond beam of the pool would be significantly widened to accommodate the rockwork's load. The beams would slope toward the ves-

Panels are fit together and shimmed up so as to match up the natural layering in the rock panels.

sel from the back edge to preserve the integrity of the shell's cages we position behind the panels before backfilling.

The pool shell would be treated with three coats of waterproofing such as Thoroseal or other types of water-proofing (see resources.) We carefully followed the label instructions, applying a single coat each day in a three-day period. Next, the panels are locked into place with steel rebar grids formed over the supporting wall. The panels are tied to the grid using the panel's steel loops which are cast into the back of each panel.

It is important that the steel be part of the pool structure not only for strength, but also to provide for proper bonding. (In cases where we need to core drill and dowel the steal into place, we run a separate bond wire from the new rebar to the watershape's bonding bus for electrical safety.

Rebar is placed in a solid filled wall and a grid schedule is made for bonding the cast rock panels to the wall.

Anchoring in Place

With this step, we anchor the panels to the supporting wall, with the exception of the threaded tie rods that extend through the face of the rock panels.

First, we place panels into place. We need to drill a hole in the panel to mark the position for mounting by using a hammer drill with a 5/8-inch drill bit. Then we insert 1/2-inch, drop-in anchor fittings through the corresponding shell hole and into the structural wall. We set the anchor with a drift pin, hammering it in which sets the expansion bullet and locks the anchor into place. Once they're all set, it's time for panel installation.

Working with four-foot panel segments will make mounting and backfilling easier. Use a 1/2-inch threaded rod and its nut and washer being inserted through the panel into the corresponding anchor. After alignments are straight, secure the rock panel to the wall using stainless steel

Holes are drilled in the panels and into the structural wall so panels can be securely anchored using all-thread bolts and nuts.

all-threaded rod, washers and nuts and then seal the anchor into place with watertight sealing caulk so as not to compromise our waterproofing layer.

Extra Support and Backfilling

If you will have any areas that are cantilevered you will need to add temporary support during the backfilling stage in the form of 2-by-4-inch wood framing. The need for this support is obvious: You will be pouring a large amount of concrete on top of the panel before we're done.

Before backfilling, however, we use rapid-set cement to lock in bottoms and sides of the rock panels. If any of the spaces between panels exceeds four inches, the gap must be bridged with wire mesh.

Filling and Finishing

In order to achieve a finished appearance, the key is blending the panel seams and hiding effectively the nuts, washers and rods.

As mentioned, the panels are joined together with quickset cement troweled into the spaces between rock panels. Once the

Once the all-thread is screwed into the threaded anchor in the wall and nuts and washers are placed on both sides of the panel, the remaining all-thread is cut off.

If any gaps greater than four inches exist between panels, lath is used to bridge the gap and prepare for seaming.

panels have been backfilled, apply a rich, one-to-one mixture of gray cement and sand, feathering it over the seams. While this cement sets, use special embossing pads to imprint details and visually blend seams with surrounding panels and textures.

This process is simple: a releasing agent is applied to the topcoat of cement that enables the installer to imprint the cement using a stamped embossing sheet --

without having the cement stick to the rubber sheet (see following section for details on blending seams.) You should pick up details from the boulder and carry small lines and cracks into the embossed area in order to hide the anchors.

After disguising the remaining anchor bolts, the rockwork will match Mother Nature's work.

Panel is securely fastened to wall with the all-thread bolt and is ready for patching and texturing over the bolt and nut

Patching and texturing the seams and exposed bolts

Steps for Specific Applications Using Cast Rock Panels

Hillside Water Feature

Prior to excavating, it's best to determine measurements with a design plan. If any shelves or waterfall exceeds 3-feet in height, engineering and planning approvals will be necessary. Outline work area with marking paint or chalk, then cut notches or steps into hillside. Over dig because expanding the area will be impossible once liner is installed.

Lay Pad of Sand

After excavation, clear area of any rocks, sharp objects, sticks, etc. Pad the ground with 2 inches of sand, this creates a cushion for the liner installation and prevents potential punctures. Pad extra rough or sharp areas with a liner underlayment, and when placing the liner on sharp rocks, smooth out sharp edges with soil cement or a similar concrete mix.

Measure and Install Liner

Measure longest length first then the widest width next. Include all vertical and horizontal areas. Allow for lots of room in your work area, this provides space for "play" in the liner so that it won't stretch when pouring protective concrete base. And just in case you need more space, allow for 5 feet outside the job area perimeter. This is important for if you have a twisting stream, you'll be tugging and moving the liner into place.

Next, lay the liner over the 2-inch pad of sand. We suggest, for "fish friendly" liner, **50 mil EDPM** for colder climates -- or **30 mil PVC**, which is not as fish friendly, but better in warmer climates and about the same cost of EDPM. Also, it is better to order liners in single sheets. To avoid risks associated with leaks caused by joints seamed on-site, know the manufacturer can fuse together liner in 7-foot sections to a size as big as half

Creating a grotto by using a cast panel turned upside down supported by a solid cast column which is "wrapped" with cast rock panels later to be back-filled with concrete.

Top panel will be further supported by a temporary 4"x4" wooden structure underneath and and the cap will be filled with concrete over a rebar grid tied into the walls and column.

A washer and nut are first threaded onto the bolt between the panel and structural wall before the bolt is threaded into the wall anchor. They will be used to hold the panel at a certain distance from the wall and the washer and nut on the front side of the panel will be tightened in order to "sandwich" and secure the panel..

an acre; larger sizes can be fusion-seamed on-site by factory representatives.

Important Note: Go overboard with anticipating a two feet extension outside the job area after making allowances for it to fill in crevices, the depth of the pond, irregular shapes, etc.

Secure Liner with Stakes

To secure the liner, place metal or wood stakes approximating every four feet around the liner's outer edges.

Float Protective Base of Concrete on Liner, Install Vertical Rebar

With the liner secured in place, float **3-4 inches** of concrete on top of the liner covering the actual work area. This will protect against leakage from punctures that might be caused by equipment, materials and crew during installation.

After floating concrete, install #4 (1/2") L-shaped rebar into the concrete. Place rebars in concrete 8-12" on center and no more than 2-3" away from the liner that hugs each vertical shelf. Don't run the rebar further than the top edge of each shelf. Allow to set overnight.

Important note: Float the concrete as far up the water feature's sides as possible, especially if you're installing GFRC boulders along the edges. Mixing fiber with concrete will greatly help in making sure it "stacks" easier and looks more "natural" in the environment.

Complete Rebar Grid, Set Panels

After the vertical rebars have set in the floated concrete base, use the horizontal steel to finish the structural grid. To set rock panels, start with whole or cut panels, work from the center of the shelf outward on either side.

About every two to three feet, drill small holes **4 inches** from the top edge of the panels. Pass tie-wire through these holes

to attach to the steel schedule. If the panels are manufactured with hooks already installed, this step won't be necessary.

Continue to cut, place and tie, and shape all vertical shelf and side surfaces in this manner.

Important note: While installing the panels, make sure the top edge of the surrounding liner is at least 3 inches above the anticipated water level.

Anchor Panels with Quick drying Cement, Install Wire Mesh, Backfill

After all vertical and side surface panels are installed, use quick drying cement ("Rock-It" is a quality quick set cement mix sold by Rock & Water Creations) at the bottom edge of each panel to secure them in place.

For large gaps on sides or between panels, cut pieces of galvanized wire mesh. Place the mesh behind the panels to cover and overlap voids. Drill holes in panel edges in order to use tie-wire to secure mesh. Rough-in large areas with quick drying cement and emboss later or, for smaller areas, rough-in and emboss at the same time.

Finally, backfill behind all vertically-mounted panels with 6-sack concrete. Be sure to use waterproofing admix material in your concrete such a Xypex (see waterproofing details and resources). Use a vibrator to ensure good settlement.

Complete Horizontal Surface Work

Where horizontal and vertical points meet, use handwork to incorporate "scrap" panel pieces at each shelf lip. For other horizontal surfaces, install whole or partial panels and/or rough areas in with cement and emboss with textured skins. Place boulders where desired throughout the water feature.

Finish Seams with Handwork and Embossing

See individual sections for details.

Pressure Wash and Color Coat, Stain and Seal

See individual sections for details.

Cast rock boulders are cut to form over walls and steps.

Reinforced Block Wall Water Feature

Important Note: *These installation directions are for when there's an existing reinforced block wall, or when one must be engineered and built due to the unusual height or weight of GFRC rock.*

Excavate Below Existing Wall or Excavate to Build New Footing and Wall

Working with the client and his/her architect or designer, determine measurements of desired water feature. Outline the work area with marking paint or chalk. Rough-in excavation for a new wall or under an existing wall. Over dig because expanding area will be impossible after installing liner. Build, or have built, footings and walls where required.

Lay Pad of Sand, Cushion Sharp Edges on Wall

See previous directions for laying pad of sand. Include an underlayment and tire patch-like "Mira Dri" to cushion the sharp edges on the wall and footing.

Measure and Install Liner

See individual step(s) from previous section.

Secure Liner with Stakes

See individual step(s) from previous section.

Float Protective Base of Concrete on Liner, Install Vertical Rebar

See individual step(s) from previous section.

Complete Rebar Grid, Set Panels

See individual step(s) from previous section.

Drill and Secure Panels to Wall

After panels are secured to the rebar grid, attach panels to the wall. Across the top third of each panel, drill 2 1/2"--deep hole with a 5/8" masonry bit, approximate. 2-3 holes. Use a razor to cut a 1-inch hole in the liner-covered wall -- cut in the center of where

Cast rock boulder cut to fit over steps or spa seating.

each drill hole lines up through the panel. Remove the liner material from cut hole, drill into the wall and set 1/2" red-head drop-in anchors as needed, tap them until they are flush and, using a drift pin and hammer, drive the bullets to expand and set the anchors.

Once holes are drilled in the panel being worked on, run a 1/2" threaded stainless rod through the panel before adding a nut and washer onto the other side. Thread them about 4 inches onto the opposite end of the rod. Now ratchet the rod into the wall anchor until tight (at this point the nut and washer will still not yet be flush with the wall) which will secure the panel.

Waterproof the hole where the liner was cut with generous amounts of Elastothane or similar mastic. Then, cut a 1/2" hole in a 3-inch square of tire patch and slide patch over the threaded rod where it meets the liner and wall. Next, hand-tighten the nut and washer over the tire patch for the final seal.

Continue to cut, place and tie, drill and waterproof panels for all vertical shelf, wall and side surfaces in this manner.

Anchor Panels with Patching Cement Mix, Install Wire Mesh, Backfill
See individual step(s) from previous section.

Complete Horizontal Surface Work
See individual step(s) from previous section.

Finish Seams with Handwork and Embossing
See individual sections for details.

Pressure Wash and Color Coat, Stain and Seal
See individual sections for details.

Pool Water Feature
Plan Locations GFRC Boulders and Panels
Determine location of boulders and rock cliff panels in advance of rebar installation and application of gunite. Note--Some areas may need professional planning in order to handle the anticipated weight loads, such as a 10' X 30' rock section.

Ensure Adequate Rebar
Stub rebar, usually up 4 feet (12 inches on center), through the bond beam to accommodate rock for each area where needed.

Waterproof Installation Sites--a **3-day** Process
Use a different color of Thoroseal for each coat (it comes in gray and white). Apply **3 coats** on area where you'll be installing GFRC rock and extend it 2 feet outside the area. You do not have to waterproof areas that will not come in contact with water. Allow **24 hours** to dry between **each** coat.

Panels are bolted to the structural wall taking care so that the natural lines of the panels will match. Bolts will later be patched over with a patching cement mixture and textured to blend with the rock panel.

double-nut on threaded rod to enable you to tighten it into the anchor. Waterproof around the anchor and threaded rod with generous amounts of Elastothane or similar mastic. Set the boulder into place and onto the threaded rod. Secure a 1/2" stainless fender washer and nut so they fit snugly against the boulder, keeping it firmly in place (be careful not to over-tighten!).

Drill and Secure Panels to Wall

See individual step(s) under "Reinforced Block Wall Water Feature" for details.

Bend Stubbed Steel, Tie Horizontal Grid, Set Panels

Bend the rebar steel stubbed up from the bond beam all the way down toward the pool bottom. Tie a horizontal grid of #4 (1/2") rebar on which to mount rock. Every two or three feet, drill small holes **4 inches** in from the top edge of the panels. Use tie-wire to pass through panels and attach to the rebar grid (this isn't necessary if panel comes ready with hooks manufactured in them).

Panels are blocked up in order to match the natural lines of the rock from one panel to the next.

To set and secure precast boulders, place the boulder in place, measure and make any necessary cuts from the rock to set "into" the side of the pool. Then reset the cut boulder into place, drill a hole with a 5/8" masonry bit through the mid-point of the rock. Insert a piece of rebar through the hole so it touches the pool wall and gently tap it to mark the spot. Remove the boulder and drill a 2 1/2"-deep hole in the pool wall where marked with the same 5/8" masonry bit. Insert a 1/2" red-head drop-in anchor, tap it until it is flush and, using a drift pin and hammer, drive the bullet to expand and set the anchor.

Tighten a 1/2 threaded stainless rod (use adequate length to extend out of the hole in the boulder). Use channel locks or

Cutting a GFRC rock panel with a concrete saw while an assistant applies water to the blade in order to lessen the dust created.

during installation. If anything is going to be built taller than 18 inches, stud in #4 (1/2") scheduled rebar, bent at 90-degree angles, into the concrete. For liner protection, duct-tape 90-degree ends to prevent puncturing liner when placing steel into wet concrete foundation. Allow to set overnight.

*Please see: **Important Note** under individual step under "Hillside Water Feature Installation."*

Liner Ponds

Grade and Excavate

Grade project area according to local codes. Remember to add **12 inches outside** the desired area because expanding will be impossible once liner is installed, and add **6 inches deeper** than desired due to the fact you will be adding 2 inches of sand and 4 inches of concrete to protect the bottom.

Lay Pad of Sand

See individual step(s) under "Hillside Water Feature" for details.

Measure and Install Liner

See individual step(s) under "Hillside Water Feature" for details.

Secure Liner Stakes

See individual step(s) under "Hillside Water Feature" for details.

Float Protective Base of Concrete on Liner

With the liner in place and secured, float **4 inches** of concrete on top of the liner covering the actual work area as a protective barrier to prevent punctures that might be caused by equipment, materials and crew

Install GFRC Boulders and / or Panels

Use your imagination with installing the panels and boulders into the embankment. Use a diamond blade saw to cut the boulders to fit into the existing contour and create a realistic positioning.

Finish Seams with Handwork and Embossing

See individual sections for details.

Pressure Wash and Color Coat, Stain and Seal

See individual sections for details.

Patching cement is applied over the seams and bolts and smoothed out to the general shape of the panels. Release powder is applied over the surface of the patch and an embossing skin is used to emboss the surface of the patch with a similar texture as the panels.

Details on Blending Seams

Pressing the embossing skin into the soft cement patch.

Handwork and Embossing

Wet Embossing Area and Apply Mixture

Moisten the area where you desire to create a natural rock impression. Use quick drying cement mixed with embossing admix, apply 1/4" to 1/2" of this hydraulic mix to the damp area with a margin trowel. Work from top down so that when you wash excess release agent off, it will not fall on areas you have already worked on.

Feather Edges

Use a semi-wet 3" paint brush to feather the outer edges, working **towards the center** for a more natural look.

Apply Release Agent

Use a common 1/2"-3/4" nap 3" paint roller, roll it in a tray of release agent. Make sure roller is covered with a generous amount of release powder. Then apply onto the texture mix area, making

sure you start at edges and roll inward. Practice in a small area first: If you use too little of powder, embossing skins (also known as texture pads) will stick and too much powder, the impressions will not be as visible.

Emboss Area with Appropriate Skin

Choose an embossing skin that resembles the texture and pattern of the adjoining GFRC panels. Using firm and even pressure, imprint the skin onto the texture mix area covered with releasing agent. Work inward from the edges, or for a vertical panel, work from top downward.

Panels are first base coated using a cement based paint.

Important Note: If you are not pleased with your initial embossing, you usually have two or three chances to re-apply the skin for a better impression. However, the drying mix probably will not accept another imprint and if you are not satisfied with the look, scrape off the mixture and restart from scratch with fresh mix and release agent.

Pressure Wash

After impressions have been made and the mix is fully cured, (usually just 3 hours depending on weather and temperatures), pressure wash the area to remove the release agent and dirt.

Remember: Test texture mix, if soft enough to scratch it with your fingernail, do not wash it yet!

Pressure washing cleans the dust, dirt and--most importantly--the release agent from the rock surface so that Pro-Seal DP-36 and color coating can be applied.

Applying Pro-Seal DP-36 to Combat Efflorescence

To guard against water migration, it is important to apply Pro-Seal's DP-36 according to manufacturer's directions. DP-36 penetrates the capillaries of the concrete and reacts with the minerals present thus forming an internal seal and hydrostatic barrier. DP-36 will not change the color, texture, or any other physical characteristics of the natural concrete surface.

Color Coating The Rock

Color Coat The Surface

To "prime" GFRC, a powdered cement-based color is mixed with an acrylic activator and coated over the work area surface with an air compressor and modified wallboard professional series hopper gun or a high volume/low pressure Model 43430 gravity feed spray gun (see Harbor Freight in Resource section). This eliminates any remaining evidence of handwork and embossing.

A speckled effect is used to create a granite look.

Protect Spray Area

Color coat will bond to almost any surface, so mask or canvas any surrounding property like

Black can be sprayed into the cracks of the rock in order to enhance the cracks. The black will not look so obvious once the color coating process is finished.

shrubs, windows, structures, and vehicles.

Mix Color Coat

Using a drill motor and paddle/paint spinner attachment, mix 1 part of an Alcantar color coat powder of your choice with 1 part Alcantar acrylic activator in a 5 gallon bucket. Mix only about a 1/2 gallon of color coat mix, for after 20 minutes, the mixture begins to thicken and clog the modified hopper gun.

Apply with Hopper Gun

Set-up the air compressor (2HP minimum) at 60-80 psi. Fill your hopper gun with the color coat mix and using one of the two smaller tips supplied with the gun, apply it to the rock surface which was previously pressure washed. Adjust the ball valve on the bottom of the hopper gun to achieve dot or mist patterns. To achieve a "dotted" pattern

Mud or floor sweep mixed with water is used to splatter the rock which masks off those areas from being coated by the next layer of color. Once the rock is coated again the masking is washed off exposing the colors below the last color coat creating a very natural rock coloring.

look, such as a granite finish, spray layers of grey and black over an oyster shell base.

Acid Stain Surface

We recommend Scofield Lithocrome Chemstains because they have eight standard colors, which can be combined, applied straight or diluted to create countless different looks. The product chemically reacts with the concrete and the color coats absorb, penetrate and become part of the surface. Also, these stains can be applied individually or as a sequence of applications, one over the other while wet. These stains will not fade, chip, crack or peel and will wear only as the concrete wears.

Process: Depending on the size of the area to be stained (see product details), dilute 2 oz. of Scofield Chemstain with 6 oz. of purified (bottled) water in a hand-held spray bottle or 2 gallon garden sprayer. Sprayers don't hold up in this process, so use cheapest sprayer available.

Producing the desired effect requires skill and experimentation. Keep in mind the appearance can be influenced by the combination or layers of Chemstain, any decoloring washes used and finishing materials applied. We suggest you work with a test section, and remember the true color will show anywhere

from 2-1/2 hours depending on the climate. Do not be afraid to experiment to achieve various effects because you can remove stain with an acid wash and start again.

Important Note: *Over the first year, expect a 20% fade and after that, the natural elements provide a unique look to the stained project.*

Decoloring Wash

To achieve a custom appearance, decoloring wash technique modifies or enhances a colored rock surface. This technique removes layers of acid stain with a less harsh mixture than the acid wash process. If done the same day, this wash can remove the majority of an acid stain. If done in subsequent days, the process is less effective.

Process: Combine 6-8 parts water to 1 part muriatic acid and 3-4 oz of liquid dish soap (to lessen acid fumes). Mix this in a 2 gallon garden or hand-sprayer, depending on the amount of area to be covered. Apply, rinse with water and check progress: continue the process until the desired effect is achieved. If mixture isn't removing coloring adequately, increase acid ratio.

Sealing

All colored surfaces must be sealed. Miracle Sealant #511 Impregnator (available through White Cap stores and Home Depot) repels moisture while allowing GFRC rock to "breathe."

Understanding "Efflorescence"

Efflorescence is a natural occurrence. It is caused by water seeping through materials and it appears on the surface of masonry work as a white crystalline or powdery deposit. This can be unsightly and undesirable so precautions are necessary (see section "Applying Pro-Seal DP-36 to Combat Efflorescence"), even though precautions are taken, efflorescence can still occur.

For efflorescence to occur, soluble salts and moisture must be present. These calcium or alkaline salts may be in the concrete, mortar, brick or cast stone, which is

Apply acid stain for final color coat.

feature is less marked until it is entirely unaffected.

Since this is usually temporary and you are dealing with soluble salts, it is recommended to let it work out through its own natural process. However, efflorescence, when compared to other stains, can be relatively easy to remove. This would entail pressure washing, re-coloring to its original condition being sure to use DP-36 in the process.

unavoidable. It is generally agreed that the dynamic process of efflorescence is when moisture enters and dissolves the salt through the walls or surface of cast stone, this combines with calcium hydroxide in the cement and brings the hydroxide to the surface in a solution that when combined with carbon dioxide, forms a white powdery substance on surface material.

Stains can also be brushed on for more control and an added texture, or dark can be added to the cracks with the brush.

Generally, in the cases when it does appear using GFRC material, the efflorescence usually decreases from year to year, so if a water feature is affected in the first year every consecutive year, the

Waterfall in the
desert by Rock and
Water Creations,
Inc.

Creating a Mud Bank
For a Stream or
Pond Edge

Mixture for a "Mud-Bank" Look

Material needed: water, cement, fiber,
decomposed granite, embossing admixture
(optional)

4:1 mix ratio

6+gallons of water
1 bag of cement
1/8lb of fiber
40-45 shovels of decomposed granite
Embossing admixture

1. In a 4.5 cubic foot mixer, add water, 1
bag of cement and fiber. Mix well.
2. Add 1/2 of the decomposed granite, mix
and check water.

3. Add and Mix-in the remaining decomposed granite, checking for sufficient water.
For vertical work, a stiffer mix is required but
should be on the wet side as soil cement (as it
is refered to for use in creating a soil or mud
bank appearance) has a short pot life.
4. Place soil cement and shape.
5. Place pebbles and float, taking care not to
set them more than 1/8" to 1/4 " deep.
6. Finish shaping soil cement and let set for
1-3 hours, depending on temperature.
7. Expose surface using a pressure washer
(1200psi minimum). Some erosion marks and
some shaping can be done at this time using a
margin trowel to cut lines and shapes. Erode
all trowel surfaces for a "natural" look.
8. Next day, wash off any remaining silt.
9. In three days, acid wash as needed using a
1:1 acid solution.

Example of GFRC Panel Construction

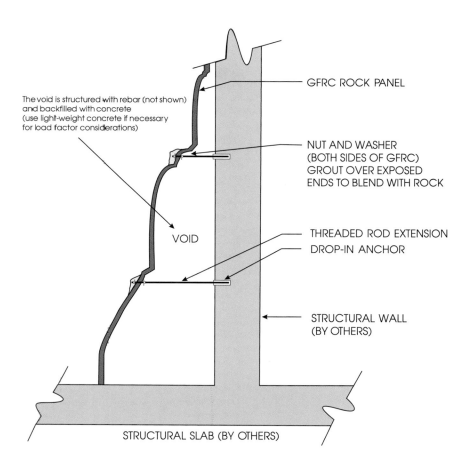

The void is structured with rebar (not shown) and backfilled with concrete (use light-weight concrete if necessary for load factor considerations)

GFRC ROCK PANEL

NUT AND WASHER
(BOTH SIDES OF GFRC)
GROUT OVER EXPOSED
ENDS TO BLEND WITH ROCK

VOID

THREADED ROD EXTENSION
DROP-IN ANCHOR

STRUCTURAL WALL
(BY OTHERS)

STRUCTURAL SLAB (BY OTHERS)

Example of Hillside Water Feature

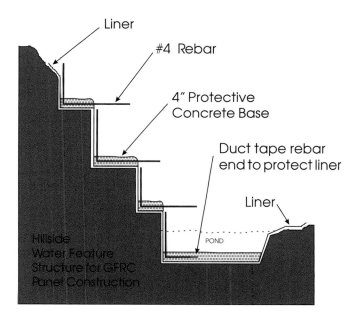

Liner

#4 Rebar

4" Protective
Concrete Base

Duct tape rebar
end to protect liner

Liner

POND

Hillside
Water Feature
Structure for GFRC
Panel Construction

Examples of Engineered Drawings

Courtesy of Miles Engineering, Van Nuys, CA, (See Resources)
Drawings are not to scale.

Waterfall Section

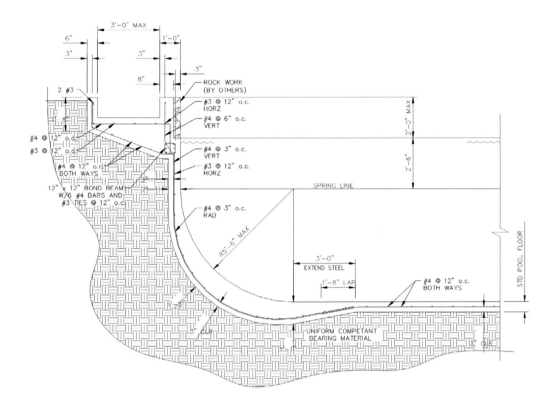

Section

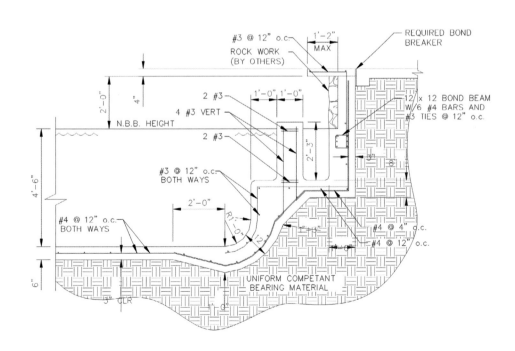

6' Slide Section

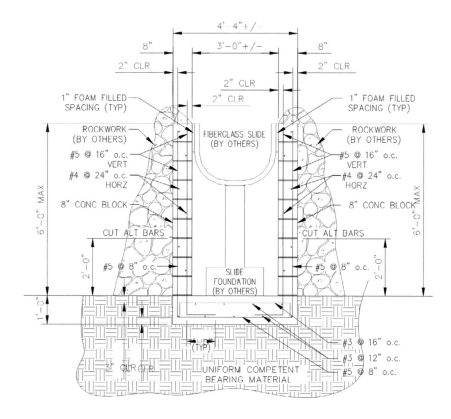

Grotto Section

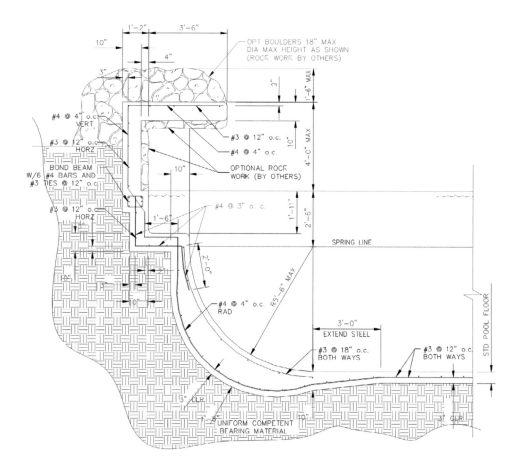

Cascading waterfall for L.A.
Zoo habitat,
by Rock and Water Creations

Resources *Part 5*

RESOURCES
Fountain, Pond, & Rock Making Supplies & Equipment

Swimming pool with waterfall, waterslide, and grotto. Private residence, Phoenix, AZ. Fabricator unknown

The following resources are a selection of those that are available, and they represent many of the major companies that supply the products used in "upscale" water features, swimming pools, spa construction, and concrete construction. We have created separate categories for each of the suppliers, depending on the majority of the products which each of the suppliers sells--some crossover will exist between them. Some of the suppliers listed are wholesale only. However, when contacted, they can give you the number of their nearest dealer, if you are not able to buy wholesale.

Cement Paints and Sealers

Alcantar Concrete Products
Color Coat, Acrylic Activator
(805) 981-9909

Degussa Building System
Thoroseal Waterproof Coating
(800) 433-9517

Miracle Sealants Company
Miracle Sealant #511 Impregnator and Mira Matte
Available at Home Depot
(800) 350-1901 ext. 3042
www.miraclesealants.com

Pro-Seal Products Inc.
Dp-36 Sealer
(800) 349-7325

RockandWater.com
World's largest supplier of artificial rock making supplies and how-to info.
Fish-safe liquid neoprene water proofing for cement
www.rockandwater.com
(417) 848-2829

Xypex Chemical Corporation
Chemical Waterproofing Admix C-1000
(800) 961-4477
www.xypex.com

Cement Pumping & Spraying Equipment

Allentown Pump & Gun
Cement Pump & Gunite Pump Manufacturers
(800) 553-3414

Quikspray, Inc.
Cement Spraying Equipment
(419) 732-2611
www.quikspray.com

Reed
Concrete Placing Equipment
(800) 541-2525

Mold Making Materials

Dow Chemical
Urethane <u>Froth-Pak</u> (Spray Foam)
(800) 735-3129

Fibermesh
Concrete Micro-Reinforcement System
(polyester fibers for reinforcing the cast rock shells)
(423) 892-7243

Magnolia Plastics, Inc
Epoxy Resins
(770) 451-2777

Moxie International
Concrete Admixtures
(800) 356-3476

Polygem
Epoxies for Worldwide Applications
(630) 231-5600

RockandWater.com
World's largest supplier of artificial rock making supplies and how-to info.
Artificial Rock Making texture pads & Mold Making Supplies
www.rockandwater.com
(417) 848-2829

Scofield
Concrete Coloring Systems and Release Agents
(800) 800-9900

Smooth-On
Flexible and Rigid Casting Resins
(800) 762-0744

Solomon Colors
Iron Oxide Pigments and Release Agents
(800) 624-0261

Precast Rock Panel Suppliers

RockandWater.com
Artificial Rock Making Supplies, How-to Info. and Large Aquarium Corals
www.rockandwater.com
(417) 848-2829

Rock & Water Creations
North America's Largest Supplier of Rock Panels
www.rock-n-water.com
(805) 524-5600

Pond and Fountain Equipment Suppliers

Aqua Ultraviolet
Ultraviolet Technology
(800) 454-2725

Fountain Supply Company
Fountain Component Supply
(661) 251-4505

J Mollema & Son Inc.
Water Gardening Supplies
(800) 224 5329

Melco Linings
Pond Liners
(714) 891-1196

Oase Pumps, Inc.
Manufacturer of decorative water feature equipment,
pumps, filtration, lighting, and specialty nozzles.
(800) 365-3880

Pond Sweep
Liner and Other Products
(630) 553-0033
www.pondsweep.com

Tetra Pond Supplies
Everything for ponds and water gardens, except the plants.
(703) 951-5400

The Fountain People, Inc.
Fountain Component Supply
(512) 392-1155

Van Ness Water Gardens
Specializing in ecosystems featuring most products and plants for
small ponds to large lakes.
(800) 205-2425

Swimming Pool Equipment Suppliers

South Central Pool Supply
"Everything But The Water"
Check the web for the nearest dealer.
www.scppool.com

Water Feature Engineering Specialists

Miles Engineering
Water Feature Engineering Specialists
(818) 994-6278

Backyard swimming pool water feature under construction with grotto, slide flume, and vanishing edge pool. By Water Features Unlimited.

List of Tools Recommended

Item	Qty	Description
1	1	Lock Box
2	1	12" Demo Saw
3	1	Hammer Drill & Bits
4	1	Jack Hammer
5	1	Rebar Cutter / Bender
6	1	Transit / Level
7	1	Compactor
8	1	1/3 Yard Mixer
9	1	Air Compressor 2 HP or Better
10	1	Skill Saw
11	1	Sawzall
12	1	Pressure Washer
13	1	Sump Pump
14	1	Concrete Vibrator
15	1	4" Metal Grinder
16	1	4" Diamond Saw
17	1	Air Blower
18	1	Heat Gun
19	1	Propane heater
20	1	Cordless Hammer Drill
21	1	1/2 Mixing Drill & Paddle
22	1	Shop Vacuum
23	2	Hopper Guns
24	1	300' Power Cords
25	1	200' Water Hose
26	2	Single Jacks
27	1	Double Jacks
28	4	Wire Pliers
29	2	Channel Lock Pliers
30	2	Robo Grip Pliers
31	2	Crescent Wrenches
32	2	Steel Shank Framing Hammers
33	2	Large Rebar Benders (Hickies)
34	4	Small Rebar Benders
35	1	6' Level
36	1	4' Level
37	1	2' Level
38	1	Torpedo Level
39	6	Margin Trowels
40	6	Wood Floats
41	4	Sponge Floats
42	2	Mag Floats
43	2	Pointed Trowels
44	4	12" Pool Trowels
45	1	Regular Rake
46	1	Landscape Rake 3'
47	2	Push Brooms
48	6	Square Shovels
49	2	Round Shovels
50	3	Madox
51	1	Pick
52	1	Digging Bar
53	4	Wheelbarrows
54	2	50 Gallon Buckets
55	10	5 Gallon Buckets
56	2	2 Gallon Garden Sprayers
57	10	Color Spray Bottles
58	2	PVC Cutters 1" / 2"
59	2	Caulking Guns
60	2	Large Sponges
61	6	Bus Trays (Embossing)
62	6	Embossing Skins / Releasing Agents
63	6	3" Paint Rollers & Covers
64	6	2" Chip Brushes
65	4	4" Chip Brushes
66	1	Gas Cans/Diesel Cans
67	1	Grease Gun
68	1	First Aid Kit
69	1ea	Dust Mask / Respirators
70	2	Tape Measures
71	2	Rubber Gloves
72	2	Leather Gloves
73	2	Thoro Seal Brushes
74	2	Scrub Brushes
75	2	Wire Brushes
76	2	Ladders

Glossary

Cascading waterfall into swimming pool, Calabases, CA by Rock and Water Creations

AAC

Autoclaved Aerated Concrete. Exceptionally light-weight precast concrete with high thermal qualities and fire resistance. Suitable for cutting with ordinary hand tools. Mix design is composed of portland cement, sand or siliceous material, lime, gypsum, finely powdered aluminum, and water. Initial mix is a combination of portland cement, sand, lime and gypsum to produce a slurry. Finely powdered aluminum mixed into a paste is added prior to placement into large, rail-like forms. The finely powdered aluminum reacts with the alkaline components of the cement and lime to produce hydrogen gas, which increases the volume approximately five times and produces a uniformly, dispersed cellular structure. Units are cut to required shape. Units are placed in an autoclave, an enclosed pressurized chamber, and steam cured at 3500 F. Approximately 80% of the ultimate volume consists of air voids.

Abrasion Resistance

The resistance of a surface against being worn away by friction or another rubbing process.

Absolute Volume

The volume of an ingredient in its solid state, without voids between individual pieces or particles. In the case of fluids, the cubic content that is occupied. In concrete, the actual volume occupied by the different ingredients is determined by dividing the weight of each ingredient by its specific gravity, times the weight of one cubic foot of water, in pounds. Example: Absolute Volume of one sack of cement equals: $94 \div (3.15 \times 62.4) = 0.478$ cubic feet.

Absorbed Moisture

Moisture which is mechanically held in a material. In aggregates, that water which is not available to become part of the mixing water is designated as "absorbed" water.

Absorption

The process by which water is absorbed. The amount of water absorbed under specific conditions, usually expressed as a percentage of the dry weight of the material.

Accelerator

An admixture which, when added to concrete, mortar, or grout, increases the rate of hydration of the hydraulic cement, shortens the time of set and increases the rate of hardening or strength development.

Adiabatic Curing

The maintenance of ambient conditions during the setting and hardening of concrete so that heat is neither lost nor gained from the surroundings of the concrete.

Admixture

A material other than water, aggregates, and portland cement that is used as an ingredient of concrete, and is added to the batch immediately before or during the mixing operation.

Adsorption Water

Water held on surfaces in a material by either physical and/or chemical forces.

Air Content

The amount of entrained or entrapped air in concrete or mortar, exclusive of pore space in aggregate particles, usually expressed as a percentage of total volume of concrete or mortar.

Air Entraining Agent

An addition to hydraulic cement, or an admixture for concrete or mortar which entrains air in the form of minute bubbles in the concrete or mortar during mixing.

Alkalis-Aggregate Reaction

Older terminology for Alkalis-Silica Reactivity (ASR).

ASR

Alkalis-Silica Reactivity. The reaction of aggregates, which contain some form of silica or carbonates with sodium oxides or potassium oxides in cement, particularly in warm, moist climates or environments, causing expansion, cracking or popouts in concrete.

Aluminous Cement

A hydraulic cement in which the principal constituents are calcium aluminates, instead of calcium silicates which comprise the major ingredients of portland cement. (See: calcium aluminate cement)

Autoclave

A chamber in which an environment of steam and high pressure is produced. Used in curing of concrete products and in the testing of hydraulic cement for soundness.

Bag (of cement)

(See: Sack)

Barrel (of cement)

A unit of weight for cement: 376 lbs. net, equivalent to 4 US bags of portland cement. The designation presently used is in tons of cement.

Blaine Fineness

The fineness of granular materials, such as cement and pozzolan, expressed as total surface area in square centimeters per gram, determined by the Blaine air-permeability apparatus and procedure.

Blast Furnace Slag

A non-metallic waste product developed in the manufacture of pig iron, consisting basically of a mixture of lime, silica and alumina, the same oxides that make up portland cement, but not in the same proportions or forms. It is used both in the manufacture of portland blast furnace slag cement and as an aggregate for lightweight concrete.

Bleeding Bleed Water

A form of segregation in which some of the water in a mix tends to rise to the surface of freshly placed concrete. Known also as water gain.

Bond

Adhesion of concrete or mortar to reinforcement, or to other surfaces. The adhesion of cement paste to aggregate.

Bush-hammer

A tool having a serrated face, as rows of pyramidal points, used to develop an architectural finish for concrete surfaces.

Calcareous

Containing calcium carbonate or, less generally, containing the element calcium.

Calcine

To alter composition or physical state by heating to a specific temperature for a specific length of time.

Calcium Aluminate Cement

The product obtained by pulverizing clinker, consisting essentially of hydraulic calcium aluminates, resulting from fusing or sintering a suitable proportioned mixture of aluminous and calcareous materials.

Capillarity

A wick-like action whereby a liquid will migrate vertically through material, in an upward direction; as oil in a lamp travels upward through the wick.

Capillary Space

In cement paste, any space not occupied by anhydrous cement or cement gel. Air bubbles, whether entrained or entrapped, are not considered as part of the cement paste.

Carbonation

1) Reaction between the products of portland cement (soluble calcium hydroxides), water and carbon dioxide to produce insoluble calcium carbonate (efflorescence). 2) Soft white, chalky surface dusting of freshly placed, unhardened concrete caused by carbon dioxide generated from unvented heaters or gasoline powered equipment in an enclosed space. 3) Carbonated, dense, impermeable to absorption, top layer of the surface of concrete caused by surface reaction to carbon dioxide. This carbonated layer becomes denser and deeper over a period of time. 4) Reaction with carbon dioxide which produces a slight shrinkage in concrete. Improves chemical stability. Concrete masonry units during manufacturing may be deliberately exposed to carbon dioxide after reaching 80% strength to induce carbonation shrinkage and to make the units more dimensionally stable. Future drying shrinkage is reduced by as much as 30%.

Cellular Concrete

A lightweight product consisting of portland cement, cement-pozzolan, cement sand, lime-pozzolan, or lime-sand pastes, or pastes containing blends of these ingredients and having a homogenous void or cell structure, attained with gas forming chemicals or foaming agents. For cellular concretes, containing binder ingredients other than or in addition to portland cement, autoclave curing is usually employed.

Cement, Portland (ASTM C150)

A powdery substance made by burning, at a high temperature, a mixture of clay and limestone producing lumps called "clinkers" which are ground into a fine powder consisting of hydraulic calcium silicates. For non-portland cements, see aluminous cement.

Cement Content

A quantity of cement contained in a unit volume of concrete or mortar, ordinarily expressed as pounds, barrels, or bags per cubic yard.

Cement Gel

The colloidal gel (glue like) material that makes up the major portion of the porous mass of which hydrated cement paste is composed.

Cementitious

Having cement-like, cementing, or bonding type properties. Material or substance producing bonding properties or cement-like materials.

Chair(s)

In concrete formwork, the support for the reinforcing steel. May also be used for spacing the backing material away from the rebar when spraying a freeform shape.

Change of State

The process whereby liquid is heated to the point of evaporation, changing the liquid into a gas. The condensation of a gas on a cooler surface, returning it from gaseous to liquid form.

Coarse Aggregate

Naturally occurring, processed or manufactured, inorganic particles in prescribed gradation or size range, the smallest size of which will be retained on a No. 4 (4.76 mm) sieve.

Coefficient of Thermal Expansion

Change in unit length per degree change of temperature.

Cold Joint

A visible lineation which forms when the placement of concrete is delayed. The concrete in place hardens prior to the next placement of concrete against it.

Colloidal

A gel-like mass which does not allow the transfer of ions.

Compressive Strength

The measured resistance of a concrete or mortar specimen to axial loading expressed as pounds per square inch (psi) of cross-sectional area. The maximum compressive stress which material, portland cement, concrete, or grout is capable of sustaining.

Concrete

A composite material which consists essentially of a binding medium, within which are embedded particles or fragments of a relative inert filler in portland cement concrete, the binder is a mixture of portland cement, possibly additional cementitious materials, such as fly ash and water; the filler may be any of a wide variety of natural or artificial, fine and coarse aggregates; and, in some instances, an admixture.

Condensation

When a moisture laden gas comes in contact with a cooler surface, a change of state from gaseous to liquid occurs.

Consistency

The degree of plasticity of fresh concrete or mortar. The normal measure of consistency is slump for concrete and flow for mortar.

Consolidation

Compaction usually accomplished by vibration of newly placed concrete to minimum practical volume, to mold it within form shapes and around embedded parts and reinforcement, and to eliminate voids other than entrained air.

Construction Joint

The contact between the placed concrete and concrete surfaces, against or upon which concrete is to be placed and to which new concrete is to adhere, that has become so rigid that the new concrete cannot be incorporated integrally by vibration with that previously placed. Unformed construction joints are horizontally placed, or nearly so.

Cure

Method of maintaining sufficient internal humidity and proper temperature for freshly placed concrete to assure proper hydration of the cement, and proper hardening of the concrete.

Density

Weight per unit volume.

Dispersing Agent

An admixture capable of increasing the fluidity of pastes, mortars, or concretes by reduction of inter-particle attraction.

Dry Rodded Weight

The weight of dry aggregate rodded into a cylindrical container of a diameter approximately equal to the height, each of 3 layers rodded 25 times, and the excess aggregate struck off level with the top of the container.

Drying Shrinkage

A decrease in the volume of concrete upon drying.

Durability

The ability of concrete to resist weathering action, chemical attack, and abrasion.

Efflorescence

A crystalline deposit of salts which leach from the concrete as soluble calcium hydroxides and within a short period of time will combine with the atmospheric carbon dioxide to form insoluble calcium carbonates, usually white in color, appearing on the surfaces of masonry, stucco or concrete.

Elastic Shortening

The shortening of a member in pre-stressed concrete which occurs on the application of forces induced by prestressing.

Entrained Air

(See: air entrainment)
Microscopic air bubbles intentionally incorporated in mortar or concrete, to improve workability and durability (usually imparting a higher degree of resistance to freezing and thawing).

Entrapped Air

Air in concrete which is not purposely en-trained. Entrapped air bubbles are normally much larger and more irregular than entrained air bubbles.

False Set

The rapid development of rigidity in a mixed portland cement paste, mortar, or concrete without the evolution of much heat. This rigidity can be dispelled and plasticity regained by further mixing without the addition of water. Premature stiffening, and rubber set are terms referring to the same phenomenon, but false set is the preferred term.

Fine Aggregate

Aggregate passing through 3/8-in. sieve and almost entirely passing a No.4(4.76 mm) sieve and predominantly retained on a No. 200 (74 micron) sieve(ASTM125).

Fineness Modulus

An index of the fineness or coarseness of an aggregate sample. An empirical factor determined by adding total percentages of an aggregate sample retained on each of a specified series of sieves, and dividing the sum by 100. Note: US Standard sieve sizes are used: No. 100, No. 50, No. 30, No. 16, No. 8, and No. 4, and 3/8 in., 3/4 in., I in., 2 in., 3 in., and 6 in.

Flash Set

The rapid development of rigidity in a mixed portland cement paste, mortar or concrete usually with the evolution of considerable heat, which rigidity cannot be dispelled nor can the plasticity be regained by further mixing without the addition of water. Also referred to as quick set or grab set.

Flexural Strength

A property of a solid that indicates its ability to withstand bending.

Fly Ash

The finely divided residue that results from the combustion of ground or powdered coal, transported from the firebox through the boiler by flue gases.

Foam Concrete

(See: Cellular concrete)

Gap-graded Aggregate

Aggregate containing particles of both large and small sizes, in which particles of certain intermediate sizes are wholly or substantially absent.

Gas Concrete

(See: cellular concrete)

GFRC

Glass Fiber Reinforced Concrete. Concrete panels, usually architectural designs, reinforced with a high zirconia (16% minimum), alkalis-resistant glass fiber. Optimum glass fiber content of 5% by weight. Lower fiber content results in lower early ultimate strengths, higher fiber content can produce composite compaction and consolidation difficulties.

Gillmore Needle

A device used in determining time of setting of hydraulic cement, described in ASTM 0 266.

Gradation

The sizing of granular materials; for concrete materials, usually expressed in terms of cumulative percentages larger or smaller than each of a series of sieve openings or the percentages between certain ranges of sieve openings.

Grout

A fluid mixture of (1) cement, sand, and water or (2) cement and water: the hardened equivalent of such mixtures.

Gunite

A term sometimes used to designate dry-mix shotcrete.

Heat of Hydration

The quantity of heat expressed in calories per gram, evolved upon complete hydration of portland cement at a given temperature.

Holding Period

Period in the manufacture of concrete products, the period between completion of casting and the introduction of additional heat or the steam curing period.

HRM

High Reactivity Metakaolin. Refined form of an ASTM C618, Class N (natural) pozzolan. A high performance, mineral admixture, similar in performance to silica fume, additionally comparable in cost. Pure white powdered in form will not effect the natural color or darken concrete as silica fume does. Suitable for high-performance color matching in architectural concrete. Dosage at 5% to 10%, of cement by weight. No bleed water, better finish ability, more creamy, easier cleanup with slightly higher 28 day strengths and 25% - 35% less plasticizer is required than with silica fume.

Process: Produced by heating a purified kaolinite clay to a specific high temperature to alter the physical composition (calcined). Through a carefully controlled refining process, impurities are removed producing an almost 100% reactive, pure white, pozzolanic powder, very evenly distributed in particle size and results in a mineral admixture which is consistent in appearance and performance from lot to lot.

Hydration

Formation of a compound by the union of water with some other substance. In concrete it is the chemical reaction between water and the cement. A concrete slab needs to completely hydrated prior to the application of paints, coatings, and flooring materials.

Hydraulic Cement

A cement that is capable of setting and hardening under water due to interaction of water and the constituents of the cement (ASTM 219).

Hydrogenesis

Another term for condensation. The term is especially applied to base and soil substrates under highway pavements, where the barometric pump causes the inhalation of humid air, which then condenses in those structures, causing an ever increasing moisture content, and sometimes instability.

Hydrologic Cycle

The Hydrologic Cycle consists of the evaporation of water from oceans and other bodies of open water; condensation to produce cloud formations; precipitation of rain, snow, sleet or hail upon land surfaces; dissipation of rain or melted solids by direct run-off into lakes and by seepage into the soil. Thereby producing a continuing endless source of water in the sub-grade.

Impermeable

The ability of a material or product to reduce or eliminate gaseous transmissions through its mass; measured as the rate of Water Vapor Transmission (WVT). Note: Not all materials that are waterproof are vaporproof; all materials that are vaporproof are inherently waterproof.

Initial Set

A degree of stiffening of the cement and water mixture. This is a degree less than final set and is generally stated as an empirical value, indicating the time in hours and minutes required for a cement paste to stiffen sufficiently to resist (to an established degree) the penetration of a weighted test needle. (Refer to ASTM C191 or C286 for weight and penetration data.)

Initial stress

In prestressed concrete, the stresses occurring in the prestressed members before any losses occur.

Jacking Equipment

In prestress concrete, the device used to stress the tendons.

Jacking Force

The temporary force exerted by the jacking device, which introduces tension into the tendons. Jacking Stress, in prestress concrete, is the maximum stress occurring in a tendon during stressing.

Keene's Cement

A finely ground high density plaster composed of anhydrous, (calcined or "dead burned") gypsum, the set of which is accelerated by the addition of other materials.

Kelly Ball

A device for determining the consistency of fresh concrete. It is sometimes used as an alternative to the slump test.

Laitance

A residue of weak and non-durable material consisting of cement, aggregate, fines, or impurities brought to the surface of over wet concrete by the bleeding water.

Lift

Layer of concrete.

Liquefaction

The change of state to a liquid. Term used instead of condensation with reference to substances which are usually gaseous.

Magnetite

An aggregate used in heavy weight concrete, consisting primarily of ferrous metaferrite (Fe_3O_4). A black magnetic iron ore with a specific gravity of approximately 5.2 and a Mohs hardness of about 6.

Marl

A calcareous clay, containing approximately 30 to 65 percent calcium carbonate (05003), found normally in extinct fresh wafer basins, swamps, or bottoms of shallow lakes.

Masonry Cement

Hydraulic cement manufactured for use in mortars for masonry construction. Normally a blend of two or more of the following materials: portland cement, natural cement, portland-pozzolan cement, hydraulic lime, slag cement, hydrated lime, pulverized limestone, talc, chalk, pozzolan, clay or gypsum; also may include air entraining additions.

Mass Concrete

Any large volume of concrete cast in place, intended to resist applied loads by virtue of its mass. Generally a monolithic structure incorporating a low cement factor with a high proportion of large coarse aggregate.

Mass Curing

Adiabatic curing, using sealed containers.

Maximum Size Aggregate

Aggregate whose largest particle size is present in sufficient quantity to affect the physical properties of concrete; generally designated by the sieve size on which the maximum amount permitted to be retained is 5 or 10 percent by weight.

Mixer

Equipment used for mixing or blending the materials used in the manufacture of concrete, grout or mortar.

Mixing Speed

Rate of mixer drum rotation or that of the paddles in a pan, open-top, or trough type mixer, when mixing a batch; expressed in revolutions per minute (rpm) or in peripheral feet per minute of a point on the circumference, at maximum diameter.

Mixing Time

For stationary mixers, mixing time is calculated in minutes from the completion of charging the mixer until the beginning of discharge; for truck mixer, time is calculated in total minutes at a specified mixing speed. The period during which materials used in a batch of concrete are combined by the mixer.

Modulus of Elasticity

A measure of the resistance of material to deformation. The ratio of normal stress and corresponding strain for tensile or compressive stresses below the proportional limit of the material; elastic modulus is denoted by the symbol "2".

Moist Room

A room used for storing and curing cementitious test specimens. The atmosphere of this room is maintained at a temperature of 73.4 3.0'F or 23.0*1.7'0 and relative humidity of at least 98 percent. These facilities must be adequate to continually maintain free moisture on the exteriors of test specimens.

Monolithic

A plain or reinforced mass of concrete cast as a single, one piece, integral structure.

Mortar

A mixture of cement, sand and water. When used in masonry construction, the mixture may contain masonry cement, or standard portland cement with lime or other admixtures, which may produce greater degrees of plasticity and/or durability.

Neat Cement

Unhydrated hydraulic cement.

Neat Cement-Paste

A mixture of water and hydraulic cement, both before and after setting and hardening.

No-Fines Concrete

A concrete mixture in which only the coarse gradation (3/8' to 3/4' normally) of aggregate issued.

Non-agitating Unit

A truck-mounted unit for transporting ready-mixed concrete short distances, not equipped to provide agitation (slow mixing) during delivery.

Non-evaporable Water

The water in concrete which is not removable by oven drying; chemically combined during cement hydration.

Ottawa Sand

A sand used as a standard in testing hydraulic cements by means of mortar test specimens. Sand is produced by processing silica rock particles obtained by hydraulic mining of the orthoquartzite situated in open-pit deposits near Ottawa, Illinois; also, naturally rounded grains of nearly pure quartz.

Over vibration

Excessive vibration of freshly mixed concrete during placement-causing segregation.

Particle-Size Distribution

Particle distribution of granular materials among various sizes; for concrete material normally designated as gradation. Usually expressed in terms of cumulative percentages smaller or larger than each of a series of sieve openings or percentages between certain ranges of sieve openings.

Pea Gravel

Portion of concrete aggregate passing a 3/8' sieve and retained on a No.4 sieve.

Peeling

A process in which thin flakes of matrix or mortar are broken away from concrete surface. Caused by adherence of surface mortar-to forms, as forms are removed, or to trowel or float in portland cement plaster.

Pining

Development of relatively small cavities in a concrete surface, due to phenomena such as cavitation or corrosion.

Plane of Weakness

The plane along which a structure under stress will tend to fracture; may exist because of the nature of the structure and its loading, by accident, or by design.

Plastic

A condition of freshly mixed concrete. mortar or cement paste indicating that it is workable and readily re-moldable, is cohesive, and has an ample content of fines and cement, but is not over wet.

Plastic Consistency

Condition in which concrete, mortar, or cement paste will sustain deformation continuously in any direction without rupture.

Plasticity

Property of freshly mixed concrete, cement paste or mortar which determines its ease of molding or resistance to deformation.

Plasticizer

A material that increases the workability or consistency of a concrete mixture, mortar or cement paste.

Porosity

The ratio of the volume of voids in the material to the total volume of the material, including the voids, usually expressed as a percentage.

Portland Blast Slag Cement Furnace

(ASTM C 595)
The product obtained by intimately intergrinding or an intimate and uniform blending a mixture of granulated blast furnace slag and portland-cement clinker.

Portland Cement

(ASTM C 150)
The product obtained by pulverizing clinker consisting essentially of hydraulic calcium silicates.

Portland-Pozzolan Cement

(ASTM C 595)
The product obtained by intimately intergrinding a mixture of portland-cement clinker and pozzolan, or an intimate and uniform blend of portland cement and fine pozzolan.

Post-tensioning

A method of prestressing concrete in which the tendons are tensioned after the concrete has hardened.

Pozzolan

(ASTM C 618)
A siliceous, or siliceous and aluminous material, which in itself possesses little or no cementitious value but will, in a finely divided form, such as a powder or liquid and in the presence of moisture, chemically react with calcium hydroxide at ordinary temperatures to form permanent, insoluble compounds possessing cementitious properties.

Precast

A concrete unit, structure or member that is cast and cured in an area other than its final position or place.

Preplaced Concrete

Concrete manufactured by placing clean, graded coarse aggregate in a form, and later injecting a portland cement-sand grout under pressure, to fill the voids.

Proportioning

Selection of proportions of material for concrete to make the most economical use of available materials to manufacture concrete of the required strength, placeability, and durability,

Prestressed Concrete

Concrete in which stresses have been introduced which are opposite in sense to those stresses that the structural member will be expected to carry during its use.

Pretensioning

A method of prestressing reinforced concrete in which the steel is stressed before the concrete has hardened, and restrained from gaining its unstressed position by a bond to the concrete.

Pumping (of Pavements)

The ejection of a mixture of water and solid materials such as clay or silt along cracks, transverse or longitudinal joints, and along pavement edges caused by downward slab movement due to the passage of heavy loads, machinery or equipment over the pavement after free water has accumulated in or on the subbase, subgrade or basecourse.

Reactive Aggregate

(See: alkalis-aggregate reaction)

Rebound

Wet shotcrete or sand and cement which bounces away from a surface again at which pneumatically applied mortar is being projected.

Refractory Concrete

Concrete having refractory properties, suitable for use at high temperatures. Calcium-aluminate cement and refractory aggregates are normally used for the manufacture of this product.

Reinforced Concrete

1. Concrete in which reinforcement, other than that provided for temperature changes for shrinkage, has been embedded in such a manner that the two materials act together in resisting forces.
2. Concrete in which steel bars have been placed to sustain the tensile stresses.

Retardation

Delaying the hardening or strength gain of fresh concrete, mortar or grout.

Retarder

An admixture which extends the setting time of cement paste, and therefore of mixtures, such as concrete, mortar, or grout.

Retempering

The addition of water and the remixing of concrete which has started to stiffen. It is usually not allowed as it may affect the ultimate strength.

Revibration

Delayed vibration of concrete that has already been placed and consolidated. Most effective when done at the latest time a running vibrator will sink of its own weight into the concrete, making it plastic and workable again.

Rock Pocket

Area or portion of hardened concrete which is deficient in mortar and consisting primarily of coarse aggregate and open voids. It is caused by insufficient consolidation or separation during placement, or both, or by leakage from form.

Rod (tamping)

A round, straight steel rod, 5/8' in diameter and approximately 24' in length, having the tamping end rounded into a hemispherical tip, the diameter of which is 5/8'.

Sack

A quantity of cement: 94 lbs. in the United States, 87.5 lbs. in Canada, for portland or air entraining portland cement, or as indicated on the sack for other kinds of cement.

Sacking

Removing or alleviating defects on a concrete surface by applying a mixture of sand and cement to the moistened surface and rubbing with a coarse material, such as burlap.

Sand

That portion of an aggregate passing a No. 4 (4.76 mm) sieve and predominantly retained on a No. 200 (74 micron) sieve.

Sand Blast

A system of abrading a surface such as concrete by a stream of sand, or other abrasive, ejected from a nozzle at high speed by water and/or compressed air.

Saponification

The deposit of a gray scum or gray dust on the inside surface of a subgrade wall or floor; as the result of moisture moving through the concrete and washing certain chemicals from the concrete mass.

Scaling

The breaking away of a hardened concrete surface, usually to a depth off 3/16".

Screed

1. Firmly placed grade strips or side forms which are set as guides for a straight edge to bring the surface of concrete to the required elevation.
2. To strike off concrete above the desired level.

Screen (or Sieve)

A metallic sheet or plate, woven wire cloth, or similar device, with regularly spaced openings of uniform size, mounted in a suitable frame or holder for use in separating material according to size.

Segregation

The tendency for the coarse particles to separate from the finer particles in handling. In concrete, the coarse aggregate and drier material remains behind and the mortar and wetter material flows ahead. This also occurs in a vertical direction when wet concrete is over vibrated or dropped vertically into the forms, the mortar and wetter material rising to the top. In aggregate, the coarse particles roll to the outside edges of the stockpile.

Set

A term used to describe the stiffening of cement paste; a condition reached by a concrete, cement paste, or mortar when plasticity is lost to an arbitrary degree, usually measured in terms of resistance to penetration or deformation. Initial set refers to first stiffening. Final set refers to attainment of significant rigidity.

Setting Time

The time required for a specimen of cement paste, mortar or concrete, prepared and tested under standardized conditions to attain a specified degree of rigidity with particular reference to initial and final setting time.

Shotcrete

Mortar or concrete conveyed through a hose and projected pneumatically at high velocity onto a surface; dry-mix shotcrete (gunite), and wet-mix shotcrete.

Sieve

See: "Screen"

Sieve Analysis

Determination of the proportions of particles of the granular material lying within certain size ranges on sieves of different size openings.

Slip Form

A form which is raised or pulled as concrete is placed. It may move vertically to form walls, stacks, bins or silos, usually of uniform cross section from bottom to top; or a generally horizontal direction to lay concrete evenly for highways, on slopes and inverts of canals, tunnels, and siphons.

Slump

A measure of the consistency of plastic concrete relative to the amount it falls when a slump cone filled with concrete is lifted vertically. The slump cone is then placed beside the specimen of concrete and the number of inches from the top of the cone to the top of the of specimen of concrete is the slump. (see: ASTM C143).

Slump Cone

A metal mold in the form of a truncated cone with a top diameter of 4", a bottom diameter of 8", and a height of 12", used to fabricate the specimen for a slump test.

Slurry

A mixture of water and such finely divided materials, such as portland cement, slag, or soil in suspension.

Spall

A fragment, usually of flaky shape, detached from a larger mass by pressure, expansion from within the larger mass, a blow, or by the action of weather.

Specific Gravity

The ratio of the weight of a material at a stated temperature to the weight of the same volume of gas-free distilled water at a stated temperature.

Stucco

A portland cement mortar material that can be applied to the surface of any building or structure to form a hard and durable covering for the exterior walls or other exterior surfaces.

Sulfate Attack

Deleterious chemical and/or physical re-action between sulfates in ground water or soil and certain constituents in cement, which result in expansion and disruption of the concrete.

Sulfate Resistance

Ability of cement paste, aggregate, or mixtures thereof to withstand sulfate attack.

Surface Moisture

Free moisture retained on the surfaces of aggregate particles which becomes part of the mixing water in the concrete mix.

Temper

The addition of water to the cement mix whether at the batch plant, during transit or at the jobsite to achieve the specified water to cement ratio.

Temperature Reinforcement

Reinforcement used to carry temperature stresses.

Temperature Rise

The increase of concrete temperature caused by heat of hydration and heat from other sources.

Tilt-up

A method of concrete construction such as where members are cast horizontally near their eventual position, usually on a recently placed slab, and then tilted into place after removal of forms.

Transit-Mixed Concrete

Concrete produced from a central-batching plant, where the materials are proportioned and placed in truck-mixers for mixing en route to the job or after arrival there.

Tremie

A pipe through which concrete may be placed under water, having at its upper end a hopper for filling, and a bale which permits handling of the assembly by a derrick.

Truck Mixer

A concrete mixer capable of mixing concrete in transit when mounted on a truck chassis.

Ultimate Strength

The maximum resistance to loads that a structure or member is capable of developing before failure occurs, or, with reference to cross sections of members, the largest axial force, shear or moment a structural concrete cross section will support.

Unit Water Content

The quantity of water per unit volume of freshly mixed concrete, often expressed as gallons or pounds per cubic yard. This is the quantity of water on which the water cement ratio is based, and does not include water absorbed by the aggregate.

Vapor Pressure

The pressure exerted by a vapor that is calculated, based upon relative humidity and temperature. The higher the humidity and higher temperature, in degrees Fahrenheit, the greater the vapor pressure exerted.

Vapor

When a liquid changes to a gaseous form. The ability of the gas to hold moisture will reduce as temperatures reduce; more moisture can be contained in the gas as the temperatures increase.

Vaporproof

A material that is totally immune to the passage of a gas under pressure. Any material that is truly vaporproof will inherently be waterproof.

Vibration

Energetic agitation of concrete to assist in its consolidation, produced by mechanical oscillating devices at moderately high frequencies.
1. External vibration employs a device attached to the forms and is particularly applicable to the manufacture of precast items and for the vibration of tunnel lining forms.
2. Internal vibration employs an element which can be inserted into the concrete, and is more generally used for cast-in-place construction.

Vicat Apparatus

A penetration device used to determine the setting characteristics of hydraulic cements.

Wagner Fineness

The fineness of materials such as portland cement expressed as total surface area in centimeters per gram, as determined by the Wagner turbidimeter apparatus and procedure.

Water-Cement Ratio

The ratio of the amount of water, exclusive of that absorbed by the aggregates, to the amount of cement in a concrete mix. Typically expressed as percentage of water, by weight in pounds, to the total weight of portland cement, fly ash, and any other cementitious material, per cubic yard, exclusive of any aggregates.

Waterproof

A material or surface that is impervious or unaffected by water in its liquid form.will repel water in its liquid form, but may not necessarily be vaporproof.

Water Vapor Pressure

The pressure exerted by water vapor. Air that contains higher amounts of water vapor exerts a higher vapor pressure than air which has a lower amount of water. In concrete, water vapor pressure is calculated by the difference between the vapor pressure of the concrete and the ambient relative humidity and temperature. The greater the difference between the water vapor and ambient humidity and temperature, in degrees Fahrenheit, the greater the water vapor pressure exerted.

Wetting Agent

A substance capable of lowering the surface tension of liquids, facilitating the wetting of solid surfaces and permitting the penetration of liquids into the capillaries.

Workability

The ease with which a given set of materials can be mixed into concrete and subsequently handled, transported, placed and finished with a minimum loss of homogeneity.

Yield

The amount of concrete produced by a given combination of materials. The total weight of ingredients divided by the unit weight of the freshly mixed concrete. Also, the cubic test of concrete produced per sack of cement. Also, the number of product units, such as block, produced per batch of concrete or sack of cement.

Contributions: Kaiser Cement, Portland Cement Association, Concrete Manual, Bureau of Reclamation, U. S. Department of the Interior, Moxie International, and other publications.

I hope you enjoyed this second edition of my book. Maybe we will see you at one of my rock making seminars.

Travel through life with love as your companion--a few sleeping nuns at your side is nice too. Take care,

J. Erik Kinkade
Author Artificial Rock Waterfalls
President, Rock and Water,
www.rockandwater.com

Notes

Book Order Form

Website orders: **www.rockandwater.com**

E-mail orders: info@rockandwater.com

Postal orders: **Rock and Water**
2631 West Bennett
Springfield, MO 65807
(417) 848-2829

Please send_____ copies of **Artificial Rock Waterfalls, Rock Making Techniques Book** and _____ copies of the companion DVD.
The price is **$59.95** per book and **$39.95** for the companion DVD. U.S. currency only.
Discount available for online purchase at **www.rockandwater.com**

Name: _____

Address: _____

              _____

              _____

Email: _____

Phone: _____

Sales tax: Please add 6.5% for books shipped to Missouri, U.S.A.

Shipping to U.S. addresses & Canada: $8.00 for the first book, $1.00 for each additional book. $9.00 for companion DVD & Book or $4.00 for shipping just the DVD (no book)

Shipping to countries outside the U.S.: $19.00 for the first book and $4.00 for each additional book. $21.00 for companion DVD & Book or $6.00 for shipping just the DVD (no book)

Payment by credit card or check:

Credit Card: VISA ____MasterCard____ Discovery___   Check____

Card Number_____   Make checks payable

Expiration Date:_____   to: Rock and Water

Name on card:_____

Signature:_____

Discounts available for multiple orders of books.

Write or e-mail for details.

www.rockandwater.com

Visit us for all of your rock making supplies, how-to info,
and pre-made artificial rock waterfalls.